SUPERBIKES

SUPERBIKES

ALAN DOWDS

tangerine Press

Author. Alan Dowds

Copyright © 2002 Amber Books Ltd

Published by Tangerine Press, an imprint of Scholastic Inc. 557 Broadway, New York, NY 10012.

10 9 8 7 6 5 4 3 2

ISBN: 0-439-42466-6

Editorial and design by
Amber Books Ltd
Bradley's Close
74–77 White Lion Street
London N1 9PF

Project Editor: Conor Kilgallon
Design: Jerry Williams

Photographs courtesy of Aerospace Publishing Ltd and Alan Dowds

Printed in Singapore

CONTENTS

Introduction

The term 'superbike' is not a new one – it was first applied to cover a genre of bikes more than thirty years ago. But the superbike of today is a very different beast from the machines of the late 1960s which began the trend for lightweight, powerful, exciting sports bikes. Modern machines such as Yamaha's YZF-R1, Honda's CBR900RR FireBlade or Suzuki's GSX-R1000 combine extremely powerful engines, producing over 110kW (150bhp), with advanced chassis technologies and incredibly low weight.

But before we examine these modern automotive masterpieces, it is worth taking a look at where they came from. Motorcycling began around the end of the nineteenth century, with various pioneering inventors marrying the then-new internal combustion engine with bicycle chassis, which had been around for

With a laid-back riding position that is perfect for leisurely cruising, the Harley-Davidson typifies the dream bike of the 1960s.

many years. Gottlieb Daimler is usually credited with producing the first powered motorcycle in 1885, with a single-cylinder four-stroke engine.

THE DECLINE OF THE BRITISH AND THE RISE OF THE JAPANESE

It was in the 1960s that motorcycling began to make the great strides forward that have led to today's machines. The motorcycle market up until then had been dominated by British motorcycle manufacturers, including Triumph, Norton and BSA. American firm Harley-Davidson and Italian firms like Ducati, Gilera and Laverda were producing their own designs, but it was British machines that formed the motorcycling mainstream.

However, the post-war decline in the fortunes of the UK firms had led to decades of under-investment in new designs and production techniques. Most British bikes were underpowered, unreliable, vibrated badly and leaked oil from their twin-cylinder engines.

Despite this, things were changing. Japanese motorcycle firms, led by Honda, began to extend their product ranges from the small-capacity commuter machines they had been making since the war, to larger capacity machinery. This threat from the east was seldom taken seriously by a complacent British bike industry, even when Japanese race teams began competing and winning at race meetings in Europe and the US.

The complacency began to evaporate when Honda released its four-cylinder CB750 in 1969, the first in a long line of successful Japanese machines. It was a massive leap forward in terms of power, refinement and reliability, and sounded a death knell for the poorly developed and produced machines of the time.

Throughout the 1970s, the 'big four' Japanese companies – Honda, Kawasaki, Suzuki and Yamaha – continued to develop and sell a wide range of motorcycles. Every year saw new advances in power and sophistication, and machines as diverse as Kawasaki's two-stroke triples, Suzuki's RE5 rotary-engine powered bike and Honda's six-cylinder CBX1000 pushed back the boundaries of engine design.

HANDLING TO MATCH THE POWER

All too often, though, the strong power of these engines overwhelmed the chassis and tyre technology of the time, and it wasn't until the early 1980s that Japanese machines began to handle well. Kawasaki's GPZ900R, introduced in 1984, was the first of the modern generation of superbikes, and its performance is still impressive today. An advanced liquid-cooled 16-valve inline-four engine produced a genuine 75kW (100bhp), and was fitted into a

Introduced in 1984, the Yamaha YZR500 won six world championships up to 1993. Rider Eddie Lawson (left) won three of them.

stiff, well-designed rolling chassis, with a full plastic fairing and less than 230kg (507lb) dry weight. It took the first three places in its maiden Isle of Man TT production race, and set the standard for other machines to follow.

The rest of the 1980s saw motorcycle engineers experiment further with turbochargers, fuel injection and large-capacity two-stroke engines, but the basic principles of modern motorcycle engines were beginning to emerge. Liquid-cooling was essential, as were four (or five) valves per cylinder. High-horsepower sportsbike applications really required four-cylinder four-strokes, and inline or V-4 engines became the dominant design. Defining bikes like Yamaha's FZR1000, Honda's CBR600 and VFR750, and Suzuki's GSX-R750 first appeared in the 1980s, and were excellent, well-designed performance machines.

By the early 1990s, however, the Japanese machines were not the only available options. European firms like Ducati and BMW began producing advanced designs. Ducati emerged from a long period of financial uncertainty, and started producing machines which were not only desirable – they were always that – but also strong performers on the road and the racetrack.

BMW, based in Munich, Germany, also began using unusual designs and more advanced engineering in its range. Bikes such as the R1100GS and K1200RS pioneered new suspension technologies, and a new range of four-valve flat-twin Boxer engines revitalized the ageing R series of tourers and sports tourers.

In England, where the troubled Triumph name was reborn in Hinckley, massive funding by property developer John Bloor had allowed a new firm to rise from the ashes of the old Triumph, with an all-new range of modern superbikes, including sports, touring and roadster machines. Powered by modern, liquid-cooled, multi-valve engines in stiff, dynamic chassis, it seemed like the British manufacturers had finally learned some lessons from the Japanese bike industry.

2000 AND BEYOND

By the end of the twentieth century, the motorcycle market had matured, and the choice for enthusiasts had never been better. Segmentation of the market, and increasingly advanced designs, meant a massive choice of excellent machinery from which to choose.

In the unlimited-horsepower 'hypersports' class, bikes such as Kawasaki's ZX-12R and Suzuki's Hayabusa brush 322km/h (200mph) while remaining civilized enough for two-up continental tours. Their untrammelled power has caused problems, though, and major manufacturers have sought to avoid statutory speed limits by adopting a 300km/h (186mph) top speed limit on these superfast machines.

The pure sportsbike class divides into three or four capacity and engine classes – 600, 750 and 1000cc fours and 1000cc V-twins. The 600 class is the most closely fought, because a 600cc motorcycle is in many ways the ideal compromise for most riders. A modern 600 like Honda's CBR600F can top 240km/h (150mph), offers superb track performance, yet remains affordable in terms of running costs and insurance. The less intense performance is also more manageable for most riders.

The 750 class has become less important on the road – most riders either go for the budget savings of a 600 or the outright performance of a 1000cc bike. But the demands of racing have always called for a 750 – the World Superbike (WSB) championship pitted 750cc four-cylinder bikes against 1000cc twins or triples throughout the 1990s, leading to the development of bikes such as Yamaha's exotic R7 and Kawasaki's ZX-7R.

The WSB championship also led to the popularity of the 1000cc sports twins

Above: The Honda CBR900 FireBlade dominated the supersports category in the 1990s.

class, which was a class of one in 1990. Ducati's 851 superbike has since grown into the latest 998 superbike, via the class-defining 916 and 996 machines. Ducati dominated WSB throughout the 1990s with its twin-cylinder machines, spurring Honda, Aprilia and Suzuki to produce their own 1000cc V-twins, although none has had the racing success of Ducati.

But the premier flagship sporting class has, until recently, been a purely road-based fight. Honda's FireBlade turned the unlimited class upside-down in 1992, and set out the essential parameters of success. It was no longer enough to produce powerful engines and fit them into chassis which worked OK on the road. Throughout the 1990s, designers had to struggle to combine the plus 93kW (125bhp) of a litre bike with the mass, dimensions and controllability of a 600cc or less machine. This intense competition has led, via Yamaha's R1 and Suzuki's GSX-R1000, to a class where the lightest weighs less than a 600cc, and the most powerful matches WSB racing machines on peak horsepower. Recent changes in racing regulations, in Moto GP and British superbikes, have revitalized racing interest in this class, however for the 2002 season BSB teams are running four-cylinder, 1000cc machines, and Moto GP1 has adopted a 990cc four-stroke class to run alongside the 500cc two-strokes.

TOURERS, TRAIL BIKES AND MARKET DEMANDS

It is not just in the sportsbike market that modern motorcycle design has excelled. Many riders use their bikes for touring, and the latest grand touring machines offer a previously unimaginable mix of luxury equipment and dynamic performance. Honda's GL1800 Gold Wing and BMW's K1200LT are amazingly complex and well-equipped machines. Technologies that had previously been seen only on sporting machines, for example aluminium frames and swingarms, weight-saving alloys and low-friction power-boosting engine internals, are now commonplace on touring bikes.

Less obvious touring machines have also become successful. The large trail-styled bikes like BMW's R1150GS and Triumph's Tiger have found favour with

Designed for the leisure market, customized cruising bikes such as this 1997 BMW Cruiser express the traditional motorcycling impulse in its purest form.

the type of 'Adventure' rider who wishes to ride hundreds of kilometres off the beaten track, including areas where road quality and condition is less than perfect. Improved performance and reliability, together with large fuel ranges and better touring equipment, have made these machines every bit as impressive as sportsbikes.

But for some riders, their touring passion must be combined with a sporting edge, and a sports-touring bike is essential. The market leaders – Honda's VFR800, Triumph's Sprint ST and Ducati's ST4 – all combine sporting chassis and engines with long-legged touring ability. Fully adjustable suspension and race-spec brakes are essential, as are plus 75kW (100bhp) engines, large fuel tanks and enough comfort and wind protection for hundreds of two-up miles in a day. The ability to ride round a racetrack on the pace the next morning is paramount.

Fuel injection and advanced electronic engine management systems have also become more commonplace across all types of machine, partly to improve performance and reduce costs, but mainly to comply with emissions legislation. Motorcycles were previously exempt from pollution checks in many parts of the world. But tightening rules mean more and more machines are following the path taken by cars a decade ago, and switching from carburettors to fuel injection.

Changing market demands have led to the expansion of several other types of machine. The budget/commuter middleweight class typified by Honda's CB600F Hornet, Yamaha's FZS600 Fazer and Suzuki's Bandit 600 have become increasingly popular. These designs use previous-generation sportsbike technologies in all-rounder roadster packages, and offer a surprisingly capable stepping-stone for novice riders, or riders on a budget looking for big-bike performance in an affordable, easy-to-use package. The custom cruiser market has also remained a strong performer in many markets, particularly the US and Germany. Image is very important in motorcycle buying decisions, and for many riders the chrome-plated, low-rider style is the purest expression of traditional motorcycling.

SUPERBIKES OF TODAY

This book attempts to give an idea of the technologies and design principles behind the superbikes of today and yesterday, placing each bike in the context of its market, and how it is used by owners. It also gives some idea of the feelings and emotions inspired by each machine, whether a gentle cruising machine, a simple commuter or a fire-breathing supersport machine.

Aprilia RS50

Aprilia's RS 50 brings big-bike styling and equipment levels to the 50cc entry class. The full fairing and race-replica paint echo the styling of the RS50's bigger brothers, while the compact two-stroke single-cylinder engine produces 6kW (8bhp) in its full-power form. The engine complies with the Euro 1 emissions limits, thanks to a catalytic converter, and also features a balance shaft for smoother running. A stiff twin-spar cast aluminium frame offers superb handling, aided by disc brakes front and rear, monoshock rear suspension and radial tyres. The advanced chassis completes the high-tech spec of an accomplished mini sportsbike. In the UK, the RS50 is usually restricted to 48km/h (30mph), so is eligible for moped status.

Top speed:	112km/h (70mph) [unrestricted]
Engine type:	49cc, l/c two-stroke single-cylinder
Maximum power:	5kW (7.3bhp)
Frame type:	twin-spar aluminium
Tyre sizes:	front 90/80 17, rear 110/80 17
Final drive:	chain
Gearbox:	six-speed
Weight:	89kg (296lb)

Aprilia RS125

Like the firm's RS50, the RS125 has a very high level of equipment, performance and styling for its class. An aluminium alloy perimeter beam frame holds an advanced liquid-cooled two-stroke engine. The 125cc single-cylinder motor uses a ceramic-type coating on the cylinder to cut friction and wear, while modern intake and exhaust designs boost power to over 194kW (260bhp)/litre. The aerodynamic fairing echoes the designs of Aprilia's GP machinery, and there have been various race-replica paint schemes. The RS125 has a high-specification chassis design, with wide, sporty tyres, 40mm (0.8in) upside-down front forks and an aluminium swingarm with adjustable monoshock rear suspension, giving fine handling especially on the track.

Top speed:	147km/h (92mph)
Engine type:	124.8cc, l/c two-stroke single-cylinder
Maximum power:	25kW (33bhp) at 11,000rpm
Frame type:	twin-spar aluminium
Tyre sizes:	front 110/70 17, rear 150/60 17
Final drive:	chain
Gearbox:	six-speed
Weight:	115kg (253lb)

Aprilia RS250

The RS250 is that increasingly rare item: a current two-stroke production roadbike. Emissions legislation worldwide has made the large-capacity two-stroke engine a thing of the past, with its poor fuel consumption and excessively dirty exhaust emissions.

But Aprilia's RS250 continues to provide some of the purest motorcycling performance available. The heart of the bike is a rather outdated engine, Suzuki's RGV250 motor, first seen in 1989. It's a V-twin two-stroke, with several advanced power-boosting features, including guillotine-type power valves, electronically-controlled 34mm Mikuni flat-slide carburettors and ceramic-coated cylinders. Aprilia modified the RGV's exhaust and intake systems to produce a power increase to 52kW (70bhp) at the crankshaft, equivalent to 280bhp/litre: the highest specific power output of any current production roadgoing motorcycle.

The rest of the bike is more than capable of handling this impressive power figure. A twin-spar aluminium frame provides super-stiff handling, and the fully-adjustable Showa upside-down front forks and rear monoshock allow a wide range of adjustment for any track or road situation. Wide sports tyres provide amazing grip, and the front twin Brembo four-piston calipers offer superlative stopping power, especially for a bike weighing just 140kg (224lb).

While the RS250's engine is based around a design that's more than a decade old,

the styling is undoubtedly modern. A banana-style upswept aluminium swingarm and twin side-mounted exhausts pay tribute to the Grand Prix technology behind the RS, as well as providing a unique look.

Since Suzuki discontinued its RGV250, the RS250 has been unique in its class. The closest rivals to this mini-racebike are the four-cylinder 400cc four stroke machines like Honda's VFR400 and Kawasaki's ZXR400. But these heavier machines can't provide the ultimate cornering experience of the RS250, nor the exhilaration of the 250's screaming two-stroke acceleration.

Top speed:	205km/h (128mph)
Engine type:	249cc, l/c 90° V-twin two-stroke
Maximum power:	52kW (70bhp) at 10,500rpm
Frame type:	twin-spar aluminium
Tyre sizes:	front 110/70 17, rear 150/60 17
Final drive:	chain
Gearbox:	six-speed
Weight:	140kg (224lb)

Aprilia Pegaso

T he Pegaso is Aprilia's entry into the popular middleweight trail-styled bike, and while the off-road capabilities of the Pegaso are limited, its long-travel suspension, off-road styled tyres and narrow chassis make it well-suited as a town and back-roads bike. Hidden behind the swoopy fairing is a modern liquid-cooled single-cylinder engine. The Rotax-based design uses a five-valve cylinder head and Sagem electronic fuel-injection to produce almost 37kW (50bhp), with a balance shaft to reduce vibration. A five-speed gearbox drives the 130-section rear tyre through a chain drive, and twin underseat silencers give a sleek tail unit design. Aftermarket hard luggage systems make the Pegaso a decent middle-distance tourer.

Top speed:	176km/h (110mph)
Engine type:	652cc, l/c single-cylinder, five-valve, SOHC
Maximum power:	37kW (49bhp) at 6250rpm
Frame type:	twin-spar aluminium
Tyre sizes:	front 100/90 19, rear 130/80 17
Final drive:	chain
Gearbox:	five-speed
Weight:	175kg (385lb)

Aprilia Blue Marlin

Unveiled at the 2001 Milan Show, the Blue Marlin is an advanced prototype model designed in collaboration with French company Boxer Design. It uses a back-to-basics approach to provide a rawer sportsbike experience. The 60º V-twin engine common to all of Aprilia's large-capacity bikes is housed in a steel-tube frame with aluminium rear plates. The line of the frame continues back up to the tail unit, in the style of race machines from the 1950s and 1960s. There are modern elements to the design too, with an aluminium tube swingarm, upside-down front forks and a purposeful twin headlamp nosecone. While the Blue Marlin looks simple, its components are very high quality, including Öhlins suspension and Brembo brakes.

Top speed:	280km/h (175mph)
Engine type:	998cc, l/c 60º V-twin, eight-valve, DOHC
Maximum power:	97kW (130bhp) at 9500rpm
Frame type:	chrome-moly steel-tube double cradle
Tyre sizes:	front 120/70 17, rear 180/55 17
Final drive:	chain
Gearbox:	six-speed
Weight:	not available

Aprilia Caponord

The large-capacity trail-styled bike market is a lucrative one in Europe, and Aprilia's entry is certainly distinctive. The large twin-headlamp fairing follows the quirky design brief of the rest of the firm's bikes, while providing good weather protection. The familiar RSV Mille-based engine has been re-tuned to produce 73kW (98bhp) rather then the 97kW (130bhp) of the donor bike, providing a flatter, less peaky power delivery, more suited to relaxing progress. The unusual 'Double Wave' frame is very stiff, and long-travel suspension soaks up the worst bumps. Like most big-bore trailbikes, the Caponord is mainly aimed at touring use, so it has a large 25-litre (5.5 gal) fuel tank, spacious pillion accommodation and a large, comfy dual seat.

Top speed:	224km/h (140mph)
Engine type:	998cc, l/c 60° V-twin, eight-valve, DOHC
Maximum power:	73kW (98bhp) at 8250rpm
Frame type:	twin-spar Double Wave aluminium/magnesium alloy
Tyre sizes:	front 110/80 19, rear 150/70 17
Final drive:	chain
Gearbox:	six-speed
Weight:	215kg (473lb)

Aprilia SLV 1000 Falco

Launched two years after Aprilia's RSV Mille, the Falco used the same 60° V-twin engine used in the RSV range. Since not every rider wishes to ride a committed sports machine like the RSV Mille, the Falco offers a more relaxed sports-touring ride. Its 998cc engine has a lower state of tune, producing 9kW (12bhp) less than the RSV Mille. But despite the lower power output and relaxed riding position, the Falco's chassis is as highly specified as the RSV. Showa upside-down forks and a Sachs rear shock are both fully adjustable, and the Brembo brakes are race-spec items. In some ways, the Falco has rather fallen between the two stools of the firm's RSV and Futura. The RSV is more suitable for track work, while the Futura is a better tourer.

Top speed:	256km/h (160mph)
Engine type:	998cc, l/c 60° V-twin, eight-valve, DOHC
Maximum power:	88kW (118bhp) at 9250rpm
Frame type:	twin-spar aluminium/magnesium alloy
Tyre sizes:	front 120/70 17, rear 180/55 17
Final drive:	chain
Gearbox:	six-speed
Weight:	190kg (418lb)

Aprilia Futura

The Futura is an attack on the lucrative sports tourer market long dominated by Honda's VFR750/800 range. Heavier and less powerful than the Falco, it combines performance and practicality with Aprilia's trademark quirky style. The single-sided rear swingarm is practical, allowing easy wheel removal, as well as stylish. The sharp-edged full-fairing design gives sound aerodynamic performance and good wind protection. The innovative exhaust incorporates a large underseat silencer making room for hard luggage provision. On the move, the retuned RSV engine allows easy progress thanks to a stronger midrange delivery, and the relaxed riding position is comfortable for hundreds of kilometres of fast touring.

Top speed:	253km/h (158mph)
Engine type:	998cc, l/c 60° V-twin, eight-valve, DOHC
Maximum power:	85kW (114bhp) at 9250rpm
Frame type:	twin-spar aluminium/magnesium alloy
Tyre sizes:	front 120/70 17, rear 180/55 17
Final drive:	chain
Gearbox:	six-speed
Weight:	210kg (462lb)

Aprilia Mille SP

The 'SP' stands for Sports Production, and the Mille SP is little more than a race bike for the road. Despite looking almost identical to the RSV Mille, nearly every part is different. The engine has a different bore and stroke, giving a smaller 996cc capacity, to allow higher revs, and there is only one spark plug per cylinder to allow bigger valves. The frame is unique to the SP, with adjustable engine position, steering head angle and swingarm pivot, and 20 per cent stiffer. The fairing is made of lightweight carbon-fibre, and the Öhlins suspension is fully adjustable. The SP was built as a 'homologation' machine, to allow the firm to race in the World Superbike championship. It was a limited-edition bike, with only 150 produced.

Top speed:	288km/h (180mph)
Engine type:	996cc, l/c 60° V-twin, eight-valve, DOHC
Maximum power:	108kW (145bhp) at 11,000rpm
Frame type:	twin-spar aluminium
Tyre sizes:	front 120/70 17, rear 190/50 17
Final drive:	chain
Gearbox:	six-speed
Weight:	185kg (407lb)

Aprilia Mille

When it first appeared in 1998, Aprilia's RSV Mille surprised many with its futuristic styling and design. The firm was known to have been working on a V-twin sportsbike for several years, but the refinement of the design impressed many observers.

The engine is a narrow-angle 60° V-twin, with four valves per cylinder. A pair of balance shafts reduce vibration from the motor, and a combination of gears and chains drive the double overhead camshafts in each cylinder head. Twin spark plugs give fast, efficient combustion, and an advanced fuel-injection system uses large 51mm (2in) throttle bodies to help produce the 97kW (130bhp) peak power.

The narrow angle of the engine allows the aluminium twin-spar frame to be compact and stiff, for dynamic handling. It also made for a shorter engine design than a 90° V-twin, allowing a sporty, short wheelbase. High-set footpegs and the slim profile of the bike give excellent ground clearance, allowing the extreme cornering angles necessary for race success. The track-spec, fully adjustable suspension at both ends, gives smooth wheel response, while the steering geometry combines quick steering with good straight line stability. Early designs wore red-painted Brembo four-piston brake calipers, but later models reverted to standard gold-finished calipers. Whatever colour they were, these calipers supplied class-leading performance.

The RSV Mille was immediately compared with Ducati's 916, another distinctive

Italian 1000cc V-twin sportsbike. While the RSV does not have the classic beauty of the red Ducati, its handling is equal to the older bike, and the RSV engine is more modern and stronger everywhere. Indeed, Ducati soon replaced the 916 with the 996, complete with a much more powerful 996cc engine.

The importance of the RSV to Aprilia cannot be overstated. Its engine has proven to be a strong, reliable unit, and the firm has been able to build a whole range of large-capacity bikes around it, well repaying the care and time taken during its development.

Top speed:	280km/h (175mph)
Engine type:	998cc, l/c 60° V-twin, eight-valve, DOHC
Maximum power:	97kW (130bhp) at 9500rpm
Frame type:	twin-spar aluminium
Tyre sizes:	front 120/70 17, rear 190/50 17
Final drive:	chain
Gearbox:	six-speed
Weight:	187kg (411lb)

Aprilia Mille R

The basic RSV Mille is a very competent bike, both for track and road use. But in 1999, Aprilia released the RSV Mille type 'R', featuring a host of modifications aimed at making it more effective on track. Outwardly, the differences are hard to spot. The 'R' has only a single seat (although a twin seat is an option). The front forks are fully adjustable Öhlins items and the rear shock is a race-spec Öhlins unit, also fully adjustable. The 'R' also wears lighter, forged aluminium Oz wheels. The engine is unchanged, but the 'R' model's chassis modifications make it much more accomplished on the race track. The 'R' is 4kg (8.8lb) lighter, and this, together with the more refined suspension, allows higher cornering speeds and quicker steering.

Top speed:	280km/h (175mph)
Engine type:	998cc, l/c 60° V-twin, eight-valve, DOHC
Maximum power:	97kW (130bhp) at 9500rpm
Frame type:	twin-spar aluminium
Tyre sizes:	front 120/70 17, rear 190/50 17
Final drive:	chain
Gearbox:	six-speed
Weight:	183kg (403lb)

Benelli Tornado

Benelli is a legendary name, with many racing successes in the past, but in recent years, it has been better known for its scooters. The appearance of the Tornado Tre 900 superbike in 1999 changed that. It uses unconventional design philosophies aimed at producing a fast, aerodynamic sportsbike, both for the road and World Superbike championship. The radiator that cools the engine is mounted under the seat, rather than in front of the engine, and this, together with the narrow three-cylinder engine, gives the Tornado a slim frontal aspect, improving aerodynamics and top speed. The 120° triple engine has a balance shaft for extra smoothness and is mounted in an innovative glued aerospace frame.

Top speed:	280km/h (175mph)
Engine type:	898cc, l/c inline-triple 12-valve, DOHC
Maximum power:	104kW (140bhp) at 11,500rpm
Frame type:	chrome-moly steel-tube/cast aluminium
Tyre sizes:	front 120/70 17, rear 190/50 17
Final drive:	chain
Gearbox:	six-speed
Weight:	185kg (407lb)

Bimota 500 V-Due

The V-Due hit the headlines when it appeared in 1997. The pioneering Italian firm had developed a direct-injection two-stroke engine, a holy grail for engine designers. Normal carburettor-equipped two-strokes are polluting and fuel-inefficient: a fuel-injected version would fix both these problems, allowing a light, powerful engine that could pass emissions laws. While the engine was innovative, the chassis was typically Bimota. An oval-tube aluminium frame provides supreme stiffness, while fully adjustable Paioli forks and an Öhlins shock give a supple, well damped ride. The V-Due could have been an amazing machine, with the handling of a 400 and power of a 750, but it was dogged by fuel-injection flaws and discontinued a year later.

Top speed:	256km/h (160mph)
Engine type:	499cc, l/c 90° V-twin two-stroke
Maximum power:	82kW (110bhp) at 9000rpm
Frame type:	aluminium twin-spar
Tyre sizes:	front 120/70 17, rear 180/55 17
Final drive:	chain
Gearbox:	six-speed
Weight:	150kg (330lb)

Bimota YB9SRI

The Bimota YB9SRi was launched in 1996 to replace the carburetted YB9SR. The SRi was unique at the time, because it was the only 600cc fuel-injected bike available, and remained so until Triumph's TT600 appeared in 2000. The SRi design was typical of Bimota's efforts at the time. The Rimini-based firm bought FZR600R and Thundercat engines from Yamaha, then installed them in the firm's own custom-built supersports chassis. A racing aluminum frame was festooned with the highest-quality chassis components available, and the engine fitted with Bimota's own intake and exhaust systems. The result was an exotic sports machine, at its best on the track, but also finished to a very high, if occasionally inconsistent, standard.

Top speed:	257km/h (160mph)
Engine type:	599cc, l/c inline-four, 16-valve, DOHC
Maximum power:	79kW (106bhp) at 12,,500rpm
Frame type:	aluminium twin-spar
Tyre sizes:	front 120/70 17, rear 180/55 17
Final drive:	chain
Gearbox:	six-speed
Weight:	175kg (386lb)

Bimota SB7

Introduced in 1994, the SB7 was a limited-edition run of 200 sports machines, powered by a version of Suzuki's GSX-R750 engine. Bimota engineers fitted the engine from the SP version of the GSX-R into a radical, aluminium beam frame. It was fitted with flatslide carburettors, but Bimota swapped these for its own electronic fuel-injection system. This helped boost drivability – often a problem with flatslide carburettors – while maintaining strong top-end power. But it is the chassis which is the most interesting part of the SB7. The massive extruded aluminium beams either side directly link the steering head with the swingarm pivot, providing a straight line for the chassis forces. This results in superlative track and road handling.

Top speed:	274km/h (170mph)
Engine type:	749cc, l/c inline-four, 16-valve, DOHC
Maximum power:	98kW (131bhp) at 11,500rpm
Frame type:	aluminium twin-spar
Tyre sizes:	front 120/70 17, rear 180/55 17
Final drive:	chain
Gearbox:	six-speed
Weight:	186kg (410lb)

Bimota Tesi

Bimota's reputation for innovation was never so strongly underlined as with this bike, built between 1991 and 1996. Based on an engineering thesis (Tesi in Italian) by its designer, Pierluigi Marconi, the Tesi was an attempt to revolutionize motorcycle front-end design by separating steering, suspension and braking forces. It uses an aluminium front swingarm with a monoshock suspension unit. This pivots to absorb bumps, but transmits braking forces directly through the arm to the bike's frame. The Tesi is steered by a 'hub centre' system. This uses a small pivot inside the wheel's hub allowing it to turn around its axle. Steering control rods on the handlebars move the wheel. The Tesi was powered by a stroked Ducati 851 engine.

Top speed:	249km/h (155mph)
Engine type:	904cc, l/c 90° V-twin, eight-valve, DOHC desmodromic
Maximum power:	84kW (113bhp) at 8500rpm
Frame type:	double aluminium plates
Tyre sizes:	front 120/70 17, rear 180/55 17
Final drive:	chain
Gearbox:	six-speed
Weight:	188kg (414lb)

Bimota SB8R

The last bike to emerge from the Rimini factory before Bimota closed its doors due to financial problems in mid-2000, the SB8R uses a tuned version of Suzuki's TL1000R engine in a high-spec supersports frame. Bimota's trademark chassis flare shines through in the SB8R, which handles much better than the TL1000R, helped by lighter weight and higher quality suspension.

The SB8R's lightweight frame is unique, using composite formed carbon-fibre plates at the swingarm pivot, bolted to the twin aluminium beams which form the main frame sections. This gives the advantages of light weight and extreme stiffness while remaining lighter than an aluminium-only part.

Italian firm Paioli supplied the full-featured suspension: both the 46mm (1.8in) upside-down front forks and the single rear shock absorber are fully adjustable for spring preload, rebound and compression damping.

The Suzuki-supplied engine uses Bimota's own fuel-injection and exhaust system to boost power. The Marelli fuel-injection throttle bodies are very large, at 59mm (2.3in), allowing the SB8R to produce more peak power than the TL1000R. Huge ram-air scoops dominate the front of the bike, channelling cool, pressurized air into the carbon-fibre airbox and increasing power at high speeds.

Perhaps the highlight of the SB8R's short life was when Australian Anthony

Gobert rode the race version of the bike – the SB8K – to victory in the wet 2000 Australian World Superbike round. Clever tyre choice saw the shoestring Bimota team beat the top factory teams by over 30 seconds – this was an astounding achievement considering the fact that the team had only received the bike five weeks previously.

Bimota also produced a special 'S' version of the SB8R, with more carbon-fibre components, including a special carbon-fibre helmet. The SB8R S weighed 2kg (4.4lb) less than the base bike.

Top speed:	272km/h (170mph)
Engine type:	996cc, l/c 90° V-twin, eight-valve, DOHC
Maximum power:	103kW (138bhp) at 9500rpm
Frame type:	aluminium twin-spar/carbon-fibre plates
Tyre sizes:	front 120/70 17, rear 180/55 17
Final drive:	chain
Gearbox:	six-speed
Weight:	178kg (392lb)

Bimota YB8

Bimota produced three variations on the YB8 between 1990 and 1994, using basically the same chassis as the previous YB6 range. The first used a Yamaha FZR1000 EXUP engine in the traditional Bimota chassis, with extremely high-quality suspension and braking components. This base model was updated in 1993 as the YB8 E. But it was a special edition of the YB8, the Furano, which most impressed. This was fitted with fuel-injection, replacing the YB8's carbs. Complete with a lighter chassis and a power increase to 123kW (165bhp), the Furano was the fastest sportsbike available when it was launched. Luckily for the owners of the 152 bikes produced, the stiff chassis provides sure handling at the huge speeds it can attain.

Top speed:	290km/h (180mph)
Engine type:	1002cc, l/c inline-four, 20-valve, DOHC
Maximum power:	111kW (149bhp) at 10,000rpm
Frame type:	aluminium twin-spar
Tyre sizes:	front 120/70 17, rear 180/55 17
Final drive:	chain
Gearbox:	five-speed
Weight:	185kg (408lb)

Bimota YB11

By the time the YB11 appeared in 1996, Bimota's Yamaha-powered range was the most well-developed in its line-up. Building on the success and relative popularity of the YB6 and YB8, the YB11 had a wheels-up revamp, but retained the same basic twin-spar chassis as the older bikes. The powerplant was now Yamaha's Thunderace engine, which the YB11 incorporates into an exquisitely designed chassis, with stiff 51mm (2in) Paioli front forks and a gorgeous single-headlight fairing. There is also an interchangeable pillion seat/tail unit which does not spoil the beautiful lines of the bike when ridden solo. Brakes are Brembo four-piston calipers, and a monoshock rear suspension system gives a firm, sporting ride.

Top speed:	280km/h (175mph)
Engine type:	1002cc, l/c inline-four, 20-valve, DOHC
Maximum power:	108kW (145bhp) at 10,000rpm
Frame type:	aluminium twin-spar
Tyre sizes:	front 120/70 17, rear 180/55 17
Final drive:	chain
Gearbox:	five-speed
Weight:	183kg (403lb)

Bimota SB6R

The SB6R followed Bimota's traditional route of taking a powerful Japanese engine from an ill-handling chassis and putting it in a better one. Mainstream Japanese sportsters mostly handled very well from the early 1990s onwards, but the 1993 Suzuki GSX-R1100 was rather overweight. Bimota took its powerful, liquid-cooled 1074cc motor and built an exotic aluminium beam chassis round it. The best wheels, suspension and brake components were bolted on, and the whole lot was swathed in gorgeous single-seat bodywork, with a stunning underseat exhaust system. The Paioli forks, Öhlins shock and Brembo brakes provide excellent handling. The only problem was the SB6R's high price and inconsistent build quality.

Top speed:	269km/h (167mph)
Engine type:	1074cc, l/c inline-four, 16-valve, DOHC
Maximum power:	116kW (156bhp) at 10,000rpm
Frame type:	aluminium twin-spar
Tyre sizes:	front 120/60 17, rear 190/50 17
Final drive:	chain
Gearbox:	six-speed
Weight:	185kg (408lb)

BMW C1

BMW is known for its unconventional designs, none more so than the C1. Safety features had never really been included on a motorbike before this machine appeared in 2000. The C1 is built around an aluminium cage, designed to keep the rider safe inside in the event of an accident. Twin seatbelts hold the rider in place, and the cage can withstand very large impacts. An impact-absorbing frontal zone helps soak up much of the energy in a head-on crash – the most common type of motorcycle crash involving other vehicles. The rest of the C1 is more conventional. The engine is a four-stroke design, with fuel-injection and automatic transmission. The C1 is offered with many accessories, including ABS, sound and luggage systems.

Top speed:	115km/h (72mph)
Engine type:	176cc, l/c single, four-valve, DOHC
Maximum power:	13kW (18bhp) at 9000rpm
Frame type:	aluminium tube space frame
Tyre sizes:	front 120/70 13, rear 140/70 12
Final drive:	belt drive
Gearbox:	automatic
Weight:	185kg (408lb)

BMW F650CS

The CS is BMW's 2002 take on the F650 Strada bike. Like the Strada, the CS is a lightweight roadster, aimed at novice motorcyclists and commuters. Based around the F650GS engine and chassis, the CS's engine shares its advanced engine management system and cylinder head design. The chassis is similar, with the exception of the road-biased wheels and tyres, and a low-maintenance belt drive. Around town, the F650CS is as easy to ride as the scooters it aims to supplant in European city centres. Soft suspension gives excellent comfort, and low-down weight distribution means good balance. Where a conventional bike has its fuel tank, the CS has an adaptable space which can hold luggage, helmet or a stereo.

Top speed:	169km/h (105mph)
Engine type:	652cc, l/c single-cylinder four-valve, DOHC
Maximum power:	37kW (50bhp) at 6800rpm
Frame type:	steel-tube cradle
Tyre sizes:	front 110/70 17, rear 160/60 17
Final drive:	Kevlar belt
Gearbox:	five-speed
Weight:	189kg (417lb) [with fuel]

BMW Funduro

The F650 was radical for BMW in several ways when it was launched in late 1993. It used chain drive, had a non-BMW Rotax engine, and was built by Aprilia in Italy. Designed to offer a smaller-capacity entry to the BMW range, the Funduro was BMW's cheapest model, and was aimed at building a mass market for the company. The advanced liquid-cooled single-cylinder engine produces a respectable 36kW (48bhp), while the trail-styled chassis has excellent round-town manners, and is capable of mild off-road use. Disc brakes front and rear are adequate rather than overwhelming, but as a commuter or first-time rider's machine, the F650 is an excellent choice. BMW also offered a more road-biased F650 Strada from 1997.

Top speed:	177km/h (110mph)
Engine type:	652cc, l/c single-cylinder, four-valve, DOHC
Maximum power:	36kW (48bhp) at 6400rpm
Frame type:	steel-tube cradle
Tyre sizes:	front 100/90 19, rear 130/80 17
Final drive:	chain
Gearbox:	five-speed
Weight:	176kg (388lb) [with fuel]

BMW F650GS

First seen in early 2000, the F650GS is an update of the F650 Funduro. Like the Funduro, it has a dual sport-road/off-road design, with a new steel-tube frame and revised engine. A new engine management system reduces pollution and improves smoothness. The bodywork is also new, and incorporates an underseat fuel tank, lowering the centre of gravity. Long-travel suspension soaks up the worst of road bumps and allows a degree of off-road use, while a tough bashplate protects the bottom of the engine. The single disc brakes front and rear are Brembo units, and there is an optional ABS anti-lock system. There is a centrestand and clock, while the twin underseat silencers are stainless steel for long life.

Top speed:	166km/h (104mph)
Engine type:	652cc, l/c single-cylinder, four-valve, DOHC
Maximum power:	37kW (50bhp) at 6500rpm
Frame type:	steel-tube bridge type
Tyre sizes:	front 100/90 19, rear 130/80 17
Final drive:	chain
Gearbox:	five-speed
Weight:	193kg (425lb) [with fuel]

BMW F650GS G-D

G-D stands for Granada-Dakar, the famous, gruelling desert rally which tests machine and rider to the limit. BMW has long been associated with this competition, and the F650GS G-D is a tribute its efforts. The engine and chassis are similar to the F650GS, with some off-road biased modifications. The G-D wears a larger 53cm (21in) front wheel, which tackles bumps and ruts more easily, while trail-type knobbly tyres cope better with mud and soft ground. The high front mudguard will not clog with mud, and the Dakar has a distinctively designed paint scheme and taller seat height. The fuel-injected F650GS engine drives through slightly lower gearing, and provides the torquey, low-down drive essential for off-road riding.

Top speed:	166km/h (104mph)
Engine type:	652cc, l/c single-cylinder, four-valve, DOHC
Maximum power:	37kW (50bhp) at 6500rpm
Frame type:	steel-tube bridge type
Tyre sizes:	front 90/90 21, rear 130/80 17
Final drive:	chain
Gearbox:	five-speed
Weight:	192kg (423lb) [with fuel]

BMW R850GS

The R850GS is the smaller-capacity companion to the R1100GS. While the R1100GS was superseded by the updated R1150GS in 1999, the R850GS remained in production as a cheaper, lower-capacity alternative. Cosmetically and mechanically, it is almost identical to the older R1100GS, the only external signs of its smaller capacity being the tank badges. The quirky styling, with a large 'snout' mudguard integrated into the top fairing, is instantly recognizable, and the screen and large tank provide good weather-protection. The flat-twin engine shelters the rider's feet and legs. Since the R850GS has all the mass of the larger 1100 model, but with less power, it offers slower progress. An ABS version is also available.

Top speed:	185km/h (115mph)
Engine type:	848cc, a/c flat-twin, eight-valve, high-cam
Maximum power:	52kW (70bhp) at 7500rpm
Frame type:	steel-tube/cast aluminium
Tyre sizes:	front 110/80 19, rear 150/70 17
Final drive:	shaft
Gearbox:	five-speed
Weight:	249kg (549lb) [with fuel]

BMW R850R

Spurred on by the success of naked retro-styled roadsters in the early 1990s, BMW used its flat-twin engine platform as the base for both the R850R and R1100R roadsters. The marriage of BMW's trademark quirky looks and retro styling is unusual, but works well. The Telelever front suspension system is clearly on display, although its wishbone and shock are cleverly incorporated into the design. Spoked wheels lend a classic air to the R, while the single-sided Paralever and clean, low-maintenance shaft drive give a tidy rear-end design. The R850R performs well for its class. High-speed riding is stymied by the naked design, but an optional screen allows relaxed motorway cruising.

Top speed:	177km/h (110mph)
Engine type:	848cc, a/c flat-twin, eight-valve, high-cam
Maximum power:	52kW (70bhp) at 7500rpm
Frame type:	steel-tube/cast aluminium
Tyre sizes:	front 120/70 17, rear 160/60 18
Final drive:	shaft
Gearbox:	five-speed
Weight:	210kg (463lb) [with fuel]

BMW R1100S

The R1100S is BMW's sportiest bike, although in comparison with other manufacturers' machinery its performance is more like a sports touring machine. Based around an uprated version of the ubiquitous BMW Boxer flat-twin engine, the R1100S motor produces a respectable 72kW (96bhp),which reaches the rear tyre through a six-speed gearbox and enclosed shaft drive.

Both the front Telelever and rear Paralever suspension systems wear lightened, uprated components, including preload adjustable front and rear monoshocks, and the R1100S has a three-part frame which uses the engine/gearbox unit as a stressed member. Brembo brake calipers are aided by BMW's Evo brake-assist system, with optional ABS. There are also optional sports handling packages available, with different suspension components and a wider back wheel.

The R1100S certainly has the most sporty styling of the BMW range. A bulbous half-fairing features an asymmetric projector lens headlight, and a pair of intakes leading to an oil cooler. The fairing continues back into the tank unit, leading to a narrow waist then out to a broad seat unit. Under the seat are two wide-bore silencers, giving the R1100S an elegant, sporty rear-end design, showing off the single-sided swingarm and taking the exhaust system out of the ground clearance equation.

Unfortunately, the engine brings ground clearance problems of its own. The flat-

twin's cylinder heads protrude a long way from the side of the bike, and committed track use can sometimes cause them to touch down in corners, necessitating carbon-fibre slider plates and suspension modifications in order to improve clearance when racing.

BMW also organized a one-make support race series, called the BoxerCup, to promote the sporting nature of the R1100S. The result has been high-quality racing, with several famous names competing, including former GP rider Kevin Schwantz and World Endurance rider Brian Morrison.

Top speed:	224km/h (139mph)
Engine type:	1085cc, a/c flat-twin, eight-valve, high-cam
Maximum power:	72kW (96.5bhp) at 7500rpm
Frame type:	cast aluminium/ steel-tube, stressed engine
Tyre sizes:	front 120/70 17, rear 170/60 17
Final drive:	shaft
Gearbox:	six-speed
Weight:	208kg (459lb) [with fuel]

BMW R1150GS

The R1150GS (Gelandstrasse, German for off-road) is the latest version of one of BMW's most successful models. This massive enduro-styled machine traces its history back to the original R80GS of 1980, and has been intensely developed since. The R80GS and R100GS used the old flat-twin engine until they were replaced in 1994 by the R1100GS, an all-new design using the firm's then-new four-valve Boxer engine.

The R1100GS had striking styling, with a large 'snout' front fairing and large fuel tank, and was an extremely successful and capable machine. But by 1999, the GS was due for an update. A larger capacity 1130cc engine was fitted, together with a six-speed gearbox and even more radical styling, including a pair of asymmetric projector beam headlights and removable screen.

The GS's unlikely-seeming combination of a large, heavy touring-bike engine and an off-road chassis offers a much more dynamic package than might be expected. BMW's trademark Telelever and Paralever suspension systems manage to combine soft, long-travel suspension with a degree of firm control not associated with trailbikes.

Strong brakes can be supplied with an ABS system, and on the move the massive weight of the GS all but disappears and the wide bars and commanding riding position allow fast, confident changes of direction.

The latest 1150 engine has a strong, torquey power delivery, and the six-speed gearbox includes an overdrive for low-rpm motorway cruising.

Pillion accomodation is admirable, and BMW offers a wide range of optional touring accessories, including hard luggage and heated grips.

Unlike most other large-capacity trail machines, BMW actively supports the use of the GS off-road, and runs training schools for its customers to teach them how to manage the hefty machine away from the Tarmac.

Top speed:	193km/h (120mph)
Engine type:	1130cc, a/c flat-twin, eight-valve, high-cam
Maximum power:	63kW (84bhp) at 6750rpm
Frame type:	three-piece, stressed engine
Tyre sizes:	front 110/80 19, rear 150/70 17
Final drive:	shaft
Gearbox:	six-speed
Weight:	228kg (503lb) [with fuel]

BMW R1150R

A larger version of BMW's R850R, the R1150R was launched in 2001 as a replacement for the R1100R. The modifications went beyond a simple capacity increase: subtle restyling and chassis modifications brought the 1150R up to date as a simple roadster for the twenty-first century. Power output is sufficient for a naked bike and the fuel-injected flat-twin engine provides strong, torquey power delivery throughout the mid-rev range. The high-cam design of the R1150R's engine, shared by all the firm's flat-twins, uses a single camshaft mounted in each cylinder block, with short pushrods leading to valve rockers. This design keeps the cylinder heads compact, improving ground clearance and making the engine narrower.

Top speed:	196km/h (122mph)
Engine type:	1130cc, a/c flat-twin, eight-valve, high-cam
Maximum power:	63kW (85bhp) at 6750rpm
Frame type:	three-piece, stressed engine
Tyre sizes:	front 120/70 17, rear 170/60 17
Final drive:	shaft
Gearbox:	six-speed
Weight:	238kg (525lb) [with fuel]

BMW R1150RS

Updated from the R1100RS in 2001, the R1150RS is a capable sports tourer with the usual BMW design parameters and equipment. The familiar 1130cc flat-twin Boxer engine is mounted in a straightforward touring chassis, with a large fairing, comfortable dual seat and comprehensive instrumentation.Though cosmetically similar to the older R1100 model, a number of changes are hidden from view. The engine has a six-speed gearbox, while the brakes use the BMW Evo system, boosting stopping power and control. An ABS system is an optional extra, as are hard luggage systems and electrically heated grips. The RS is lighter and more sporty than BMW's larger tourers, such as the R1150RT, but has lower equipment levels.

Top speed:	200km/h (124mph)
Engine type:	1130cc, a/c flat-twin, eight-valve, high-cam
Maximum power:	70kW (94bhp) at 7500rpm
Frame type:	three-piece, stressed engine
Tyre sizes:	front 120/70 17, rear 170/60 17
Final drive:	shaft
Gearbox:	six-speed
Weight:	246kg (542lb) [with fuel]

BMW R1150RT

The RT is the luxury touring option from BMW's 'R' series of flat-twin powered machines. Sitting between the R1150RS and the K1200LT, it provides almost as much comfort and equipment as the LT in a smaller, more manageable package. Based, like the R1150RS, around a 1130cc Boxer engine, the RT boasts extensive weather-cheating bodywork, with a large headlight that incorporates twin integral foglights. An electrically operated windscreen allows on-the-move adjustment, and optional luggage and stereo sound systems enhance long-distance pleasures. Pillion accomodation is spacious and comfortable. The RT features BMW's integral ABS Evo brakes, mating advanced ABS with electrohydraulic servo-assistance.

Top speed:	217km/h (135mph)
Engine type:	1130cc, a/c flat-twin, eight-valve, high-cam
Maximum power:	71kW (95bhp) at 7250rpm
Frame type:	steel-tube/cast aluminium
Tyre sizes:	front 120/70 17, rear 170/60 17
Final drive:	shaft
Gearbox:	six-speed
Weight:	279kg (615lb) [with fuel]

BMW K1200LT

This range-topping flagship bike is the ultimate BMW touring bike. Aimed at providing similar luxury to the firm's 7-series cars, the K1200LT combines outstanding comfort, weather protection and equipment with ample long-distance performance. From the comfy seat, the rider is assailed by a barrage of meters, gauges and controls, including a trip computer, stereo radio/CD and cruise control, as well as the usual fuel level, engine temperature, engine rpm and gear position. The massive weight of the LT is disconcerting at first, but once moving, it is relatively easy to manoeuvre. The engine's smooth delivery makes fast progress a pleasure and the suspension makes an excellent job of controlling the LT's mass on the move.

Top speed:	208km/h (130mph)
Engine type:	1171cc, l/c inline-four, 16-valve, DOHC
Maximum power:	73kW (98bhp) at 6750rpm
Frame type:	cast aluminium
Tyre sizes:	front 120/70 17, rear 160/70 17
Final drive:	shaft
Gearbox:	five-speed
Weight:	345kg (759lb) [with fuel]

BMW K1200 RS

Launched in 1997, the K1200RS is a true heavyweight sports tourer. The most powerful BMW motorcycle available, the RS is powered by an inline-four, 1171cc four-cylinder engine mounted horizontally along the bottom of the bike. Bosch Motronic electronic fuel-injection supplies accurately metered fuel, and a catalytic convertor in the exhaust cleans up emissions to below legal limits. Producing 97kW (130bhp), the K1200RS engine is also used in the K1200LT tourer, and is the latest 16-valve version of the long-running K series of engines, which first appeared in the K100 eight-valve design of the early 1980s.

A full sports-touring fairing encloses the engine and chassis in a slippery aerodynamic plastic cocoon. The rider is similarly protected: the broad screen guides windblast up and around the rider and pillion, and scoops below the fuel tank allow the rider's legs to tuck in. The RS is also adjustable to suit: the screen, seat, handlebars and footpegs are all movable to exactly fit riders of different sizes.

Like the rest of BMW's large-capacity bikes, the K1200RS uses the firm's Telelever front suspension system. This wishbone-type arrangement uses a single combined damper/spring unit, connected to the front suspension tubes by the large cast aluminium strut. The Telelever system separates the suspension from braking forces, which are resolved through the cast strut, rather than through sprung telescopic forks. The benefits of Telever are considerable on a fast, heavy machine like the K1200RS: conventional forks would have to be so firm to prevent excessive

dive under braking that they would be very uncomfortable over bumps. The rear suspension is the usual Paralever single-sided shaft-drive arrangement common to BMW's large-capacity machines.

The latest version of BMW's ABS EVO front brakes ensure safe, rapid stopping even under difficult conditions. Optional accessories, such as heated grips and luggage systems, can turn the K1200RS into an even more capable grand tourer. The sports part of the equation is less obvious – at 285kg (627lb), the K1200RS is too heavy to offer anything like modern sportsbike performance.

Top speed:	256km/h (160mph)
Engine type:	1171cc, l/c inline-four, 16-valve, DOHC
Maximum power:	97kW (130bhp) at 8750rpm
Frame type:	cast aluminium
Tyre sizes:	front 120/70 17, rear 170/60 17
Final drive:	shaft
Gearbox:	five-speed
Weight:	285kg (627lb) [with fuel]

BMW R1200C

This curious-looking bike was intended to marry the high-tech design principles of BMW's bike range with the chrome-clad styling of a traditional cruiser bike. Based around a 1170cc version of the firm's well-proven flat-twin Boxer engine, the R1200C's unconventional looks bely its modern performance.

The air/oil-cooled engine provides plenty of grunty power, delivered through a Paralever single-sided shaft-drive swingarm to the fat, spoked rear-wheel. A Bosch fuel-injection system ensures smooth, economical running and a catalytic converter in the stainless steel exhaust cuts harmful pollution. The R1200C has a five-speed gearbox, driven through a car-type dry plate clutch.

The front end is typically BMW: the firm's wishbone-type Telelever suspension uses a single shock absorber system to give stiff yet compliant feedback from the 46cm (18in) front wheel. The suspension is proudly displayed on the R1200C, rather than hidden behind a fairing as on BMW's touring and sport-touring models. An advanced ABS II system is an option, giving an extra safety margin to the Brembo front calipers.

But it is the styling that dominates the bike. Chrome plate abounds, and details like the single seat with fold-down backrest/pillion pad and chrome sideplates show a bold, retro style, not dissimilar to the firm's Z3 sports car range. Long pullback handlebars give a traditional cruiser riding position, and aftermarket accessories

including leather saddlebags and different handlebars allow owners to customize the R1200C to their own tastes.

On the move, the low seat, forward footpegs and 'apehanger' handlebars make for an unusual riding position, and the R1200C really needs an aftermarket screen for comfort on longer journeys.

It was the R1200C that saved James Bond from certain death in the action movie 'Tomorrow Never Dies' in 1997, performing a number of unlikely stunts in the process.

Top speed:	253km/h (115mph)
Engine type:	1170cc, a/c Boxer twin, eight-valve, high-cam
Maximum power:	45kW (61bhp) at 5000rpm
Frame type:	aluminium spine, with engine as stressed member
Tyre sizes:	front 100/90 18, rear 170/80 15
Final drive:	shaft
Gearbox:	five-speed
Weight:	236kg (519lb) [with fuel]

Buell XB9R
Firebolt

Buell's founder, Erik Buell, has always provided innovative design solutions in his bikes, and the Firebolt is no exception. Like all Buells, the Firebolt uses a Harley-Davidson engine (Buell is owned by Harley) in a short, sportsbike chassis.

But hidden inside this chassis are a few surprises. The hollow aluminium twin-spar frame doubles as the fuel tank, while the rear swingarm is also hollow, holding the oil tank for the dry-sump engine. These unique designs save space and weight, allowing the Firebolt a featherweight 175kg (386lb) claimed dry weight, as well as an ultra-short 1320mm (52in) wheelbase. The space created above the engine by the unconventional fuel tank allows a large-volume airbox, further boosting power and torque.

The rim-mounted front brake is also a first on a production bike, and is designed to give stronger power and better cooling. The power from the six-piston caliper biting on the huge 375mm (15in) disc means only one disc and caliper is needed, further saving unsprung weight. This also helps the fully-adjustable Showa suspension give a well-damped, compliant action, as well as improving acceleration. It also means braking forces are not transmitted through the wheel's spokes, allowing a lighter wheel design.

The Harley-based engine is a 45° V-twin with a curious mix of technology. Even though it uses air-cooling and pushrod overhead valve actuation – both now

outdated technologies – it has an advanced, modern fuel-injection system to improve power and drivability while meeting tough emissions laws. Air ducting, large cooling fins and a fan keep the rear cylinder cool despite being hidden behind the frame, and the large-capacity silencer, essential to reduce noise emissions, is hidden away underneath the engine behond a stylish bellypan.

There is a small, stylish twin-headlamp fairing which carves through the wind, and the instruments are housed in a lightweight magnesium dash, underlining Buell's determination to shed weight from every component possible.

Top speed:	232km/h (145mph)
Engine type:	984cc, a/c 45° V-twin, four-valve, OHV
Maximum power:	69kW (92bhp) at 7200rpm
Frame type:	aluminium twin-spar
Tyre sizes:	front 120/70 17, rear 180/55 17
Final drive:	Kevlar belt, with idler tensioner
Gearbox:	five-speed
Weight:	175kg (385lb)

Buell X1 Lightning

Buell's X1 Lightning is a rather unconventional sportsbike. Few bike designers would choose the Harley-Davidson 1203cc Sportster engine as the base for a sports machine – the dated engine suffers from excess vibration and low specific power output. But Buell has managed to produce an unexpectedly dynamic machine. The engine receives a 50 per cent power boost over the base design thanks to fuel-injection, a free-flowing exhaust and other modifications. The engine is fitted via vibration-absorbing mounts to a short, lightweight steel-tube frame. Showa upside-down forks and underslung rear shock offer firm sports-style suspension, while a large single front disc and six-piston caliper provide strong stopping power.

Top speed:	280km/h (175mph)
Engine type:	1203cc, a/c 45° V-twin, four-valve, OHV
Maximum power:	75kW (101hp) at 6000rpm
Frame type:	chrome-moly steel-tube perimeter
Tyre sizes:	front 120/70 17, rear 170/60 17
Final drive:	Kevlar belt
Gearbox:	five-speed
Weight:	200kg (440lb)

Cagiva Mito 50

In most parts of Europe, 50cc machines can be ridden some years before riders are old enough to ride large-capacity machines, so the market for stylish, race-styled machines is very competitive. The Mito 50 certainly fits the bill – its twin-spar frame, upside-down front forks and monoshock rear suspension look exactly like the equipment on larger machines. And while the tiny 49cc two-stroke engine produces less than 7.5kW (10bhp), it still offers plenty of fun, due to the minute all-up weight of the Mito. The Mito 50 has to compete with practical scooter-styled machines, so incorporates a useful helmet storage area under the fake fuel tank. The real fuel tank is under the seat. It is almost identical to the Spanish Derbi GPR50 sports moped.

Top speed:	97km/h (60mph)
Engine type:	49.9cc, l/c two-stroke single
Maximum power:	7kW (9bhp) at 9000rpm
Frame type:	twin-spar steel
Tyre sizes:	front 90/90 16, rear 120/80 16
Final drive:	chain
Gearbox:	six-speed
Weight:	87kg (192lb)

Cagiva Mito 125

Basically a racing 125cc bike for the road, the Mito packages gorgeous, big-bike styling (it looks almost identical to Ducati's 916), with a high-specification sportsbike chassis and engine. Its single-cylinder two-stroke engine produces around 22kW (30bhp) – a typical output for this class, but still impressive in bhp per litre terms at 179kW (240bhp) per litre. The chassis is also typical, if well-appointed. A twin-spar aluminium frame is more than stiff enough for the Mito's power, and the upside-down front forks and rear monoshock are well-damped, if a little soft for heavier riders. The gull-wing-type swingarm is copied from GP bikes, and allows clearance for the large expansion chamber exhaust.

Top speed:	160km/h (100mph)
Engine type:	124.6cc, l/c single-cylinder two-stroke
Maximum power:	23kW (31bhp)
Frame type:	aluminium twin-spar
Tyre sizes:	front 110/70 17, rear 150/60 17
Final drive:	chain
Gearbox:	six-speed
Weight:	129kg (285lb)

Cagiva River

A rather rare machine from Italian manufacturer Cagiva, the River is a simple, unassuming commuter machine with some pleasing design touches. Powered by an elderly single-cylinder air-cooled engine, the River's moderate power and economical running makes it ideal for commuting. The River is also cheap to insure and eligible for the limited A1 licence class in Europe. The chassis is rather higher-spec, with a twin-spar frame, upside-down forks and monoshock rear, while Brembo disc brakes front and rear ensure trouble-free stopping. A small screen and stylish sculpted fuel tank increase the River's appeal, and it could also be supplied with factory-approved hard luggage panniers, further enhancing its commuter role.

Top speed:	161km/h (100mph)
Engine type:	601cc, a/c single, four-valve, SOHC
Maximum power:	25kW (34bhp) at 6000rpm
Frame type:	aluminium twin-spar
Tyre sizes:	front 110/80 17, rear 140/70 17
Final drive:	chain
Gearbox:	five-speed
Weight:	160kg (353lb)

Cagiva Raptor 650

Hot on the heels of Cagiva's TL1000-powered Raptor 1000 came this smaller, middleweight version. First introduced in 2000, the Raptor 650 is cosmetically identical to its larger sibling, but is powered by a Suzuki SV650 engine. This liquid-cooled V-twin powerplant also looks very similar to the larger TL1000 engine, making the Raptor 650 and 1000 difficult to tell apart at a glance. But differences there are. Predictably, the smaller-engined bike is much less powerful, with less exhilirating performance, though conversely it is considerably lighter than the 1000cc bike and has more nimble handling and braking. The twin 298mm (11.7in) front disc brakes are very strong, while a narrower 160-section rear tyre allows quicker steering.

Top speed:	209km/h (130mph)
Engine type:	645cc, l/c 90° V-twin, eight-valve, DOHC
Maximum power:	52kW (70bhp) at 9000rpm
Frame type:	steel-tube trellis
Tyre sizes:	front 120/70 17, rear 160/60 17
Final drive:	chain
Gearbox:	six-speed
Weight:	180kg (397lb)

Cagiva V-Raptor 650

The V-Raptor 650 is basically a Raptor 650 with a small nosecone fitted. This largely cosmetic bodywork makes little difference to the bike's top speed and gives no real weather-protection to the rider, but together with the removable carbon-effect seat cowl it does give the V-Raptor a radically different look. On the road, the V-Raptor feels almost identical to the plain bike, although it steers slightly quicker thanks to some small adjustments to the steering geometry and wider handlebars. The 43mm (1.7in) Marzocchi upside-down front forks give excellent feedback from the sporty radial tyre, while the Sachs rear shock is longer than the Raptor's item, raising the back of the motorcycle.

Top speed:	212km/h (132mph)
Engine type:	645cc, l/c 90° V-twin, eight-valve, DOHC
Maximum power:	52kW (70bhp) at 9000rpm
Frame type:	steel-tube trellis
Tyre sizes:	front 120/70 17, rear 160/60 17
Final drive:	chain
Gearbox:	six-speed
Weight:	185kg (408lb)

Cagiva Gran Canyon 900

Cagiva and Ducati have a close history – once part of the same group – and the Gran Canyon is a product of the former close relationship. Powered by the long-running air-cooled V-twin that powers Ducati's 900SS, the Gran Canyon was Cagiva's entry in the important large trailbike market until 2000. The Ducati-supplied engine is fitted with Cagiva's own airbox and exhaust, and the Weber-Marelli fuel-injection adjusted to suit. The engine's Desmodromic valves allow strong performance, but are tricky to maintain. The Gran Canyon has an attractive, striking design. The neat bodywork makes it look much smaller than some of its competitors. The long travel suspension works well on road, though the front brakes are marginal.

Top speed:	190km/h (118mph)
Engine type:	904cc, a/c 90° V-twin, four-valve, desmodromic SOHC
Maximum power:	48kW (64bhp) at 7400rpm
Frame type:	steel-tube cradle
Tyre sizes:	front 110/80 19, rear 150/70 17
Final drive:	chain
Gearbox:	six-speed
Weight:	218kg (480lb)

Cagiva Navigator

The Navigator is based on Cagiva's Gran Canyon trailbike, but with the engine replaced by Suzuki's TL1000 engine. Cagiva's own exhaust and intake system has produced an engine with lower peak power than the TL1000R, or Cagiva's own Raptor 1000 (which also uses the TL engine). But the Navigator is still one of the most powerful trail-styled bikes available, and is comparatively light, giving it sharp performance. The V-twin engine allows for a narrow chassis and low air resistance for higher top speed. But while the small front-fairing looks good, it does not offer as much protection as some of the Navigator's larger competitors. The soft suspension and strong brakes just about keep up with the engine.

Top speed:	224km/h (140mph)
Engine type:	996cc, l/c 90° V-twin, eight-valve, DOHC
Maximum power:	72kW (97bhp) at 8400rpm
Frame type:	steel-tube trellis
Tyre sizes:	front 110/80 18, rear 150/70 17
Final drive:	chain
Gearbox:	six-speed
Weight:	210kg (463lb)

Cagiva V-Raptor 1000

Designed by the same man who penned the Ducati Monster, Miguel Angel Galluzzi, the V-Raptor is a typically Italian design. Based around a steel-tube frame and a rebadged Suzuki TL1000R engine, it is a direct competitor to the Monster 900. The engine is much more powerful than Ducati's air-cooled 900, and Cagiva's fuel-injection and exhaust systems provide smooth power delivery. Strong, grunty power throughout the rev range makes the V-Raptor great fun on the road, catapulting it out of bends, front tyre skipping over the road surface. The obvious difference between this and the Raptor 1000 is the bodywork. A radical nosecone arches over the wide handlebars then merges back into the front of the fuel tank.

Top speed:	237km/h (147mph)
Engine type:	996cc, l/c 90° V-twin, eight-valve, DOHC
Maximum power:	79kW (106bhp) at 8500rpm
Frame type:	steel-tube trellis
Tyre sizes:	front 120/70 17, rear 180/55 17
Final drive:	chain
Gearbox:	six-speed
Weight:	197kg (434lb)

Cagiva
Xtra-Raptor

Launched in 2001, this factory-built special is based around a higher-specification V-Raptor, and is a limited production model of 999 units, each having a numbered plaque on the top yoke. All bodywork is finished in carbon-fibre, which contrasts with the dark grey of the headlight fairing. Both the front forks and the rear monoshock are fully adjustable, and the rear shock itself is a new design which adds 50mm (2in) to the rear ride height. This has the effect of sharpening the steering still further, and shortening the wheelbase by 10mm (0.4in). To counter any possible instability from the steeper steering, the Xtra Raptor has a neat steering damper, installed parallel with the lower yoke.

Top speed:	237km/h (147mph)
Engine type:	996cc, l/c 90° V-twin, eight-valve, DOHC
Maximum power:	79kW (106bhp) at 8500rpm
Frame type:	steel-tube trellis
Tyre sizes:	front 120/70 17, rear 180/55 17
Final drive:	chain
Gearbox:	six-speed
Weight:	197kg (434lb)

Cagiva Raptor 1000

The naked-style city bike has long been popular in Europe, and with unique design elements it can command a premium price. Ducati led the way with its Monster range in 1993, and Cagiva has moved the sector on with the Raptor, fittingly designed by Miguel Galluzzi, father of the Monster design. The Raptor 1000 uses Suzuki's TL1000 engine in a classy roadster chassis, which oozes Latin design. From the angular steel-tube frame to the sharp, teeth-like footrest hangers and the muscular fuel tank, this is an exceptionally stylish machine. It also has the performance to back-up the style. The TL engine has been revised for better low-down performance, and the Raptor also has lower gearing, for strong acceleration.

Top speed:	237km/h (147mph)
Engine type:	996cc, l/c 90° V-twin, eight-valve, DOHC
Maximum power:	79kW (106bhp) at 8500rpm
Frame type:	steel-tube trellis
Tyre sizes:	front 120/70 17, rear 180/55 17
Final drive:	chain
Gearbox:	six-speed
Weight:	192kg (423lb)

CCM 604e Sport

CCM, based in the north of England, was originally a competition off-road manufacturer, until it turned its hand to leisure-based machines in 1998. It builds a range of off-road, enduro and Supermoto bikes, based around a Rotax-built single-cylinder engine. The 604e Dual Sport is a road-legal enduro machine, which is equally at home on or off road, its high-quality, long travel WP suspension giving superb damping and feedback. Though long in the tooth, the engine is still capable of exhilirating acceleration and strong low-down grunt, especially matched with the tiny all-up weight of the 604. Many riders fit the factory-option 43cm (17in) road wheels and tyres, turning the 604 into a full-bore, continental-style Supermoto.

Top speed:	145km/h (90mph)
Engine type:	598cc, a/c single-cylinder, four-valve, SOHC
Maximum power:	40kW (53bhp) at 7500rpm
Frame type:	steel-tube double cradle, oil in frame
Tyre sizes:	front 90/90 21, rear 120/90 18
Final drive:	chain
Gearbox:	five-speed
Weight:	132kg (291lb)

Ariel Square Four

The Ariel Square Four, or 'Squariel' as it became known, is unique among classic machines. Both four-cylinder engines and 1000cc capacities are rare in the classic world, but this bike had both. Unveiled in 1930 as a 498cc design by Edward Turner, it evolved over the years into a 996cc machine, and the last of the approximately 4000 bikes produced came off the Birmingham assembly line in 1958. The engine used a twin crankshaft design, with two pushrod-operated overhead valves per cylinder. The exhaust ports exited out of either side into aluminium exhaust manifolds, leading to either a single- or twin-downpipe per side. A large single Solex carburettor feeds the combustion chambers, and starting is by kick lever.

Top speed:	153km/h (95mph)
Engine type:	996cc, a/c square-four, eight-valve, OHV
Maximum power:	26kW (35bhp) at 5400rpm
Frame type:	steel-tube cradle
Tyre sizes:	front 3.25 x 19, rear 4.00 x 18
Final drive:	chain
Gearbox:	four-speed
Weight:	197kg (434lb)

Benelli
SEI 750

The Benelli company began life in a small Italian town in 1911 as a general engineering business. In the early 1970s it began producing four- and six-cylinder machines, including the 750 and 900 sixes or Sei. The Sei 750 was not the most powerful machine in its class, but the straight-six engine gave it an undeniable appeal. Three Dell'Orto carburettors feed the 12-valve air-cooled motor, which delivers its 52kW (70bhp) through a five-speed gearbox to the rear wheel. A typical 1970s chassis is based on a steel-tube frame, with conventional front forks and twin shock rear suspension. The Sei 750 makes a useful touring machine: the engine is smooth, the 22-litre (4.8 gal) fuel tank allowing well over 240km (150 miles) between refills.

Top speed:	182km/h (113mph)
Engine type:	747cc, a/c inline-six, 12-valve, SOHC
Maximum power:	53kW (71bhp) at 8900rpm
Frame type:	steel-tube double cradle
Tyre sizes:	front 100/90 18, rear 120/90 18
Final drive:	chain
Gearbox:	five-speed
Weight:	219kg (483lb)

Honda
CB 400 Four

The CB400 Four is a little jewel of a motorcycle, produced in the café racer style from 1975 to 1977. Its single overhead-cam inline-four engine is a conventional, two-valve per cylinder design, but the small dimensions of the engine internals allow it to rev to a dizzy-for-the-time 10,000rpm.

The 408cc engine was developed from the CB350F powerplant, which had been rather underpowered for many riders. Though n ot an overly powerful motorcycle, the CB400's 28kW (37bhp), combined with a 178kg (392lb) dry weight, gives the little 400 exceptional performance for its capacity. The motor was extremely smooth, as well as willing, and was fairly reliable, although its high-revving nature occasionally caused piston-ring wear. Screw and locknut valve adjustment and points ignition meant regular maintenance was required for optimal running.

Chassis technology in the mid-1970s was more than up to dealing with the little 400, a conventional telescopic front fork and twin-shock rear suspension offering plush damping. Although the steel-tube double cradle frame now looks rather spindly, it was just about stiff enough for good handling. A single front brake disc and a single-leading-shoe rear drum brake allowed reliable stopping, and starting was by electric button and kickstart.

But is was the CB400's styling that won many fans, particularly the serpentine

chromed downpipes of the four-into-one exhaust, which culminate in a glorious chrome collector box and megaphone silencer. A slabby fuel tank holds just 14 litres, but the CB400's meagre fuel consumption means this will still carry the rider past 240km (150 miles) between fuel stops.

Although the CB400 Four was a successful design, it was soon replaced by cheaper, less impressive parallel twin machines, such as the three-valves per cylinder CB400 Dream and later Super Dream. However, these designs did not have the style, panache or performance of the little 400 Four.

Top speed:	167km/h (104mph)
Engine type:	408cc, a/c inline-four eight-valve, SOHC
Maximum power:	28kW (37bhp) at 9000rpm
Frame type:	steel-tube cradle
Tyre sizes:	front 90/90 18, rear 110/90 18
Final drive:	chain
Gearbox:	six-speed
Weight:	178kg (392lb)

Honda CB750 Four

In many ways, the inspiration for all modern superbikes, the CB750 is an important bike for several reasons. At its launch in 1969, it was the most advanced motorcycle available – its single overhead cam, eight-valve inline-four engine is unremarkable now, but was in a class of its own in 1969. An electric start, front disc brake (a first on a production machine) and a smart four-into-four exhaust system completed the impression of a high-tech flagship machine, which waslight years ahead of the slow-revving British twins which represented its competitors.

The inline-four engine at the heart of the CB was the only four-cylinder bike engine in production at the time. It used horizontally split crankcases with a built-up roller bearing crankshaft, dry sump lubrication and a single chain-driven camshaft. The cylinder dimensions were undersquare, with a bore and stroke of 61 x 63mm (2.4 x 2.5in), and a duplex chain transmitted the primary drive from the crank to the multiplate wet clutch.

A five-speed gearbox drove the spoked 46cm (18in) rear wheel via a roller chain, which had its own mechanically driven oil pump, which constantly dripped lube on to the chain while the bike was moving. Four individual Keihin slide carbs fed the engine with fuel/air mix.

If the CB750's engine was revolutionary, the frame was less radical. A simple steel-

tube cradle design, it was designed more as a platform on which to mount all the other components than as a dynamic chassis component. While it was stiff enough, the handling it provided was less impressive than some of the CB's less illustrious competitors. Similarly, the exotic hydraulic disc brake was not much more powerful than contemporary high-performance twin-leading-shoe drum brakes.

But it was the all-round package that made the CB750 so impressive, as well as its affordable price and outstanding reliability. It was also the first sign of developments to come from the Japanese manufacturers.

Top speed:	280km/h (115mph)
Engine type:	736cc, a/c inline-four, eight-valve, SOHC
Maximum power:	49kW (66bhp) at 8000rpm
Frame type:	steel-tube double cradle
Tyre sizes:	front 3.25 x 19, rear 4.00 x 18
Final drive:	chain
Gearbox:	five-speed
Weight:	219kg (482lb)

Honda CBX1000

There were several six-cylinder bikes in the 1970s, including Benelli's Sei, and the Kawasaki Z1300. Honda's entry was the CBX1000, which was an impressive, well-engineered design. Honda had dabbled with six-cylinder machines before, in racing. The most notable was the RC-165 250 inline-six, the designer of which, Shoichiro Irimajiri, masterminded the CBX1000 project. The original CBX1000 was a sporting machine. The inline-six engine was designed like a racebike motor, with light valve-gear and 24 valves. A steel-tube backbone frame hangs the engine below it, and the cylinders are canted forward to give space for the rider's legs. Six chromed exhaust header pipes curve back, ending in two large megaphone silencers.

Top speed:	225km/h (140mph)
Engine type:	1047cc, a/c inline-six, 24-valve, DOHC
Maximum power:	78kW (105bhp) at 9000rpm
Frame type:	steel-tube spine
Tyre sizes:	front 100/90 19, rear 120/90 18
Final drive:	chain
Gearbox:	five-speed
Weight:	247kg (545lb)

Kawasaki KH500

Kawasaki's early 1970s sportsbike range was dominated by light, powerful two-stroke triples: from the 250cc S1 through to the fearsome H2 750cc, the KH500 being a suitable midway point. Developed from the earlier H1, the original triple of 1969, the KH500 had a piston-ported two-stroke engine in a steel-tube cradle frame. Conventional if rather insubstantial suspension and braking components were marginal on the earlier H1, but improved in later models. Later models also tended to gain weight over the originals, and the engines were re-tuned for less ferocious power. By the late 1970s, the poor fuel consumption, reliability and handling of the triples made them less popular, and they were replaced by newer four-stroke designs.

Top speed:	190km/h (118mph)
Engine type:	498cc, a/c inline-triple, two-stroke
Maximum power:	39kW (52bhp) at 7000rpm
Frame type:	steel-tube cradle
Tyre sizes:	front 3.25 x 19, rear 4.00 x 18
Final drive:	chain
Gearbox:	five-speed
Weight:	192kg (423lb)

Kawasaki Z1

Kawasaki was preparing to produce a 750cc inline-four sportsbike in 1969, but its plans were interrupted somewhat by Honda's CB750, introduced that year. Kawasaki put its own superbike on hold, then when it saw the success of the Honda, revised the project with even higher aims.

The result, released in 1972, was the 903cc Z1. An amazingly well-specified machine for its time, the big Kawasaki was the fastest, most powerful machine available, with a high-performance double overhead cam eight-valve engine. Four 28mm (1.1in) Mikuni carburettors supplied the fuel/air mix to the 8.5:1 compression ratio cylinders, and a stylish four-into-four exhaust system sounded as good as it looked.

Unfortunately, the chassis wasn't nearly as accomplished. A simple mild-steel-tube cradle frame simply wasn't stiff enough to handle the engine's power, and this unstable foundation wasn't helped by skinny front forks and unsophisticated twin rear shocks. The Z1 had a pronounced weave at high speeds, although careful, smooth riding minimized its effects.

The single hydraulic front brake disc was rather marginal, as many 1970s designs were, and it was worse in the wet, although the large rear drum was a useful backup. Later European models came with a second front disc, and Kawasaki offered a twin disc conversion kit for sportier riders.

The Z1 was an instant success among sportbike riders who prized outright power above handling, and its handsome styling and sleek lines were no handicap in the showroom.

Later models lost a small amount of top-end power, as well as details like the automatic chain oiling pump. But the basic Z1 engine lasted well beyond the model's demise in 1978, forming the basis for a whole range of air-cooled eight-valve engines, right up to the GPz1100 of 1985 and the 1100 Zephyr of 1992. Its strong bottom end and easy tuning also made it a popular choice for drag-racers.

Top speed:	216km/h (134mph)
Engine type:	903cc, a/c inline-four, eight-valve, DOHC
Maximum power:	61kW (82bhp) at 8500rpm
Frame type:	steel-tube double cradle
Tyre sizes:	front 3.25 x 19, rear 4.00 x 18
Final drive:	chain
Gearbox:	five-speed
Weight:	230kg (506lb)

Laverda Jota

The original Jota was a UK-only special, produced around the basic Laverda 3C production bike. The UK importer, Roger Slater, built a road version of his successful racing 3C, with sporting camshafts, pistons and exhausts. The bike was so successful that the Italian Laverda factory itself began producing the Jota. The heart of the Jota is an inline-triple engine, with a 180° crankshaft. This design has the big end journals arranged so that when the two outside pistons are at the top of their stroke, the centre piston is at the bottom. This gives a unique sound, although it makes the engine vibrate heavily. The Jota was the fastest superbike of its time and, unlike many competitors, it handled well, due to Brembo brakes and Marzocchi suspension.

Top speed:	209km/h (140mph)
Engine type:	981cc, a/c inline-triple, six-valve, DOHC
Maximum power:	67kW (90bhp) at 7500rpm
Frame type:	steel-tube double cradle
Tyre sizes:	front 4.10 x 18, rear 4.25 x 18
Final drive:	chain
Gearbox:	five-speed
Weight:	241kg (532lb) [with fuel]

Norton Commando 850

The last of the Norton parallel twin machines, the Commando began life as a 750 in the late 1960s, growing into the 829cc 850. Its most interesting feature was its ingenious engine mounting system. Norton had neither the time nor money to develop a new engine to take on modern superbikes like Honda's CB750, and was stuck with the parallel twin engine from the Atlas. This engine was powerful enough, but suffered from terrible vibration. Norton decided to use a system of rubber mounts between the engine and frame, while mounting the swingarm to the engine casings. This 'Isolastic' mounting system kept the swingarm true in relation to the engine position, while isolating the rest of the chassis from the intrusive vibes of the engine.

Top speed:	185km/h (115mph)
Engine type:	829cc, a/c parallel twin, four-valve, OHV
Maximum power:	45kW (60bhp) at 6000rpm
Frame type:	steel-tube double cradle
Tyre sizes:	front 4.10 x 19, rear 4.10 x 19
Final drive:	chain
Gearbox:	five-speed
Weight:	195kg (430lb)

Suzuki RG500

It was 1985 when Suzuki launched the RG500 Gamma, a machine which became one of the firm's most legendary names. Essentially a road-going version of the company's RG500 GP bike, the Gamma is powered by a compact, square four cylinder two-stroke engine. This unusual design is essentially two parallel twin engines combined into one, with the two crankshafts geared together.

The engine's disc-valve intake system is also unusual. This design uses thin metal discs on the ends of the crankshafts, with slots cut out. As the engine turns, these slots pass in front of the side-mounted carburettors, allowing the engine to draw fuel/air mix into the lower crankcase. From there, the mixture is forced by the descending piston through transfer ports into the combustion chamber, as in other two-stroke designs. Disc valve induction gives strong power delivery, although the carburettor and airbox installation is made difficult by the position of the inlets on either side of the engine. Aprilia's 250 Grand Prix bikes have also used disc-valve induction.

The RG engine also has a power-boosting AEC exhaust valve system. This electrically operated device opens a valve in the exhaust port at around 7500rpm, uncovering a small chamber which alters the exhaust characteristics to give both strong mid-range and top-end power.

This GP-style engine is mounted into a then-radical race-replica chassis. The frame

is constructed of square-section aluminium tubing in a cradle arrangement, making it very stiff and light. The air-adjustable front suspension incorporates an adjustable anti-dive damping system, while the rear monoshock is operated by an aluminium swingarm linkage, and is preload-adjustable. The four-piston front brakes worked well for 1985, but have since been overtaken in performance.

As has the rest of the RG500. Its fire-breathing mid-1980s performance is little better than some modern 400s, and is outclassed in terms of performance and handling by a bike like Suzuki's own GSX-R600.

Top speed:	217km/h (135mph)
Engine type:	498cc, l/c square four, two-stroke
Maximum power:	71kW (95bhp) at 9500rpm
Frame type:	aluminium double cradle
Tyre sizes:	front 120/70 17, rear 180/55 17
Final drive:	chain
Gearbox:	six-speed
Weight:	154kg (340lb)

Suzuki GT750

Introduced in 1971, the GT750 was Suzuki's attempt to match the Honda CB750 and Kawasaki two-stroke triple sports machines. Although it had a very high specification, with a powerful liquid-cooled engine, it performed better in a touring role. The engine, developed from the firm's air-cooled two-strokes, is piston-ported, and its water-cooling system was the first on a production bike for 40 years. It breathes through three 32mm (1.3in) Mikuni carburettors, and the exhaust is a three-into-four design, the centre downpipe splitting into two silencers.
The original bike had a large front drum brake, while later models had twin hydraulic discs, which worked well in dry, but suffered from lag in wet conditions.

Top speed:	193km/h (120mph)
Engine type:	738cc, l/c inline-triple, two-stroke
Maximum power:	50kW (67bhp) at 6500rpm
Frame type:	steel-tube double cradle
Tyre sizes:	front 3.25 x 19, rear 4.00 x 18
Final drive:	chain
Gearbox:	five-speed
Weight:	214kg (472lb)

Ducati Monster 600 Dark

The 600 Dark is a basic, entry-level version of Ducati's Monster roadster. The Monster 600 is powered by a 583cc air-cooled V-twin engine, which has desmodromic valve actuation. This desmo system uses a pair of rockers to forcibly close as well as open the engine's poppet valves, rather than using springs to close the valves. The Dark is a low-spec budget machine. The paintwork is all matt-finish black, rather than gloss, and the unsophisticated chassis is low on equipment, while the engine is rather weak with indifferent mid-range and wheezy top-end power. In its favour though, the Monster 600 steers well, and the single front Brembo disc brake offers acceptable feel and power. The Monster 600 Dark is ideal for novices.

Top speed:	183km/h (114mph)
Engine type:	583cc, a/c 90° V-twin, four-valve, desmodromic SOHC
Maximum power:	38kW (51bhp) at 8000rpm
Frame type:	steel-tube trellis
Tyre sizes:	front 120/60 17, rear 160/60 17
Final drive:	chain
Gearbox:	five-speed
Weight:	174kg (383lb)

Ducati Monster 620ie

Like its larger 900cc sibling, the Monster 600 found itself lacking in terms of power against new late-1990s competition. Suzuki's SV650 and Cagiva's Raptor 650 are both much more powerful than the elderly 583cc Ducati design, and the mini-Monster needed an update. The 620ie was Ducati's response. A larger stroke crankshaft increased capacity by 35cc, and a new fuel-injection system replaced the 600's carburettors, improving power delivery and cutting emissions. Ducati also upgraded the rest of the bike with twin front brake discs and improved dash and electrics. An 'S' version of the 620ie is also available, with aluminium swingarm, small headlight fairing, ride-height-adjustable rear shock and carbon-fibre body panels.

Top speed:	193km/h (120mph)
Engine type:	618cc, a/c 90° V-twin, four-valve, SOHC desmodromic
Maximum power:	45kW (60bhp) at 9500rpm
Frame type:	steel-tube trellis
Tyre sizes:	front 120/60 17, rear 160/60 17
Final drive:	chain
Gearbox:	five-speed
Weight:	177kg (389lb)

Ducati 748
Biposto

First launched in 1994, the 748 was a smaller-capacity version of the 916 introduced the year before. The 748 was similar in many ways – the frame, suspension and brakes were largely identical to the larger bike. The maximum power output was not much less either, at 73kW (98bhp) compared to 81kW (109bhp) for the original 916. Perhaps surprisingly, the 748 felt markedly different on the road. The more highly tuned 748cc engine had to be revved higher for the same power output, and this revvy nature tended to make the rider feel more involved in the riding experience. Minor chassis differences – mostly different tyre sizes – give a different feel on the road, and many consider the 748 to be the better steering machine.

Top speed:	248km/h (154mph)
Engine type:	748cc, l/c 90° V-twin, eight-valve, DOHC desmodromic
Maximum power:	73kW (98bhp) at 11,000rpm
Frame type:	steel-tube trellis
Tyre sizes:	front 120/60 17, rear 180/55 17
Final drive:	chain
Gearbox:	six-speed
Weight:	200kg (441lb)

Ducati 748R

By 2000, the 748 range was due for an overhaul, and Ducati took the decision to expand the range at the entry level. Consequently, three 748s were launched in late 1999. The base 748E was a budget, entry-level model, with cheaper chassis components and the same engine as used in the previous 748 Biposto. The middle bike of the range was the 748S, which used the older engine design but had uprated wheels and suspension.

But the star of the 2000 748 lineup was undoubtedly the 748R. This racer-for-the-road incorporated a number of changes to improve the 748's chances in World Supersport racing. A new frame, borrowed from the 996 WSB machine, allowed the use of a new, larger airbox. This in turn allowed an all-new fuel-injection setup, with Formula One-style 'shower' fuel injectors mounted deep inside the airbox, pointing straight into the massive 54mm (2.1in) throttle bodies.

Together with higher lift cams and large valves, these changes transformed the performance of the 748 engine, boosting power to 79kW (106bhp), and giving increased potential for power increases on racing machines.

The chassis was also radically overhauled. New, lightweight Marchesini wheels reduced unsprung weight and increased style. Fully adjustable Showa suspension front and rear is highly specified, with a gold-coloured titanium-nitride coating on the fork stanchions to reduce stiction and improve performance.

For 2001, the 748R received a further update. The Showa suspension was replaced with race-spec Öhlins forks and rear shock, and a lighter frame was fitted.

Detail engine refinements improved drive and reliability and a carbon-fibre airbox added extra stiffness to the lightweight frame.

The 748R riding experience is sublime. Best kept for track riding, the feedback and response from the chassis, together with the strong engine, makes riding the 748R one of the purest sportsbike experiences available.

Top speed:	254km/h (158mph)
Engine type:	748cc, l/c 90° V-twin, eight-valve, DOHC desmodromic
Maximum power:	79kW (106bhp) at 11,500rpm
Frame type:	steel-tube trellis
Tyre sizes:	front 120/60 17, rear 180/55 17
Final drive:	chain
Gearbox:	six-speed
Weight:	192kg (423lb)

Ducati 750 F1 Racing

Based around the successful TT2 race bike, the first 750 F1 was introduced in 1984 as this race machine, to compete in the TT1 class and endurance races. The 600cc engine of the TT2 was increased in capacity to 748cc, and although the 750 F1 wasn't as successful as the TT2, it evolved into a replica roadbike. The first 750 F1 appeared in 1985, using a steel-tube trellis frame, cantilever rear suspension and cast wheels. The suspension and braking components offered decent performance for the time, but the 41cm (16in) front wheel limited tyre choice, and the F1 road bike was less impressive than many Ducati fans had hoped. Three special editions were released, the Montjuich in 1986, the Laguna Seca in 1987 and the Santa Monica in 1988.

Top speed:	260km/h (175mph)
Engine type:	748cc, a/c 90° V-twin, four-valve, SOHC desmodromic
Maximum power:	47kW (63bhp) at 7500rpm
Frame type:	steel-tube trellis
Tyre sizes:	front 120/80 16, rear 130/80 18
Final drive:	chain
Gearbox:	five-speed
Weight:	175kg (386lb)

Ducati Monster 750

Filling the gap between the Monster 600 and 900, the Monster 750 uses the 750SS engine in an 888-derived frame and SS suspension package. Introduced in 1996 with a single front brake disc and carburettors, the specification has gradually been uprated to the current twin front disc, fuel injected version. The 750 has all the style and handling performance of the smaller Monster 600, while its larger engine offers a more satisfying power delivery, almost as much as the 900, but with lower cost and less weight. The stiff frame and firm suspension give a sporty ride, and wide handlebars and a low centre of gravity allow easy, nimble handling. Around town, the Monster 750 is a handsome performer, but not so composed on longer trips.

Top speed:	193km/h (120mph)
Engine type:	748cc, a/c 90° V-twin, four-valve, SOHC desmodromic
Maximum power:	48kW (64bhp) at 8500rpm
Frame type:	steel-tube trellis
Tyre sizes:	front 120/60 17, rear 160/60 17
Final drive:	chain
Gearbox:	five-speed
Weight:	179kg (394lb)

Ducati 750SS

The 750SS has an illustrious past, as far back as the 750 Sport of 1970. The basic layout of an air-cooled desmodromic-valve 90° V-twin first appeared as a 750, later growing into the 900, and later into the water-coled superbikes. The latest 750SS is a pleasing mix of traditional and modern technology. The rather elderly engine design isn't the most powerful available, but has been modernized with a reliable, smooth electronic fuel-injection system. With the firm, narrow chassis, the torquey, low-revving twin is most at home on flowing, twisty backroads, where its lazy power delivery supplies surprisingly quick progress. The suspension units are basic, but high-quality items, and the Brembo front brakes are very effective.

Top speed:	201km/h (125mph)
Engine type:	748cc, a/c 90° V-twin, four-valve, SOHC desmodromic
Maximum power:	48kW (64bhp) at 8500rpm
Frame type:	steel-tube trellis
Tyre sizes:	front 120/70 17, rear 160/60 17
Final drive:	chain
Gearbox:	five-speed
Weight:	181kg (400lb)

Ducati 851

By 1985, Ducati needed a new generation of engine. Its two-valve desmodromic V-twins had performed well, but were becoming less successful in racing. Young Italian engineer Massimo Bordi's thesis was on a four-valve desmodromic design, and he soon produced the first prototype of the new Ducati engines. The design was incredibly advanced, borrowing heavily from F1 car technology, and incorporated liquid-cooling and fuel-injection, as well as the four-valve Desmoquattro heads. After showing promise in some races, an 851cc version was produced which evolved into the 851 superbike. Mounted in a steel-tube trellis frame, with an aluminium swingarm and Marzocchi suspension, the first 851s appeared in 1987.

Top speed:	240km/h (149mph)
Engine type:	851cc, l/c 90° V-twin, eight-valve, DOHC desmodromic
Maximum power:	78kW (105bhp) at 9000rpm
Frame type:	steel-tube trellis
Tyre sizes:	front 120/70 17, rear 180/55 17
Final drive:	chain
Gearbox:	six-speed
Weight:	180kg (397lb)

Ducati 888

The 888 was a natural development of the 851 superbike, and emerged from the many SP customer racer bikes which Ducati built – the 851SP engine had been an 888cc design since 1990. The 888 Strada appeared in 1992 and replaced the 851 until the 916 appeared in 1994. A refinement of the 851, the 888 Strada was heavier, and though it produced slightly less power, performance and top speed were similar. The styling was more coherent, but the Desmoquattro Ducati was still some way from the gorgeous, evocative styling of the later 916/748 family. Road riding was improved by the lower state of engine tune, while a more powerful alternator and less expensive suspension components also pointed towards a road bike.

Top speed:	246km/h (153mph)
Engine type:	888cc, l/c 90° V-twin, eight-valve, DOHC desmodromic
Maximum power:	75kW (100bhp) at 9000rpm
Frame type:	steel-tube trellis
Tyre sizes:	front 120/70 17, rear 180/55 17
Final drive:	chain
Gearbox:	six-speed
Weight:	210kg (463lb)

Ducati Monster 900

The Monster range, together with the Desmoquattro superbike range, has been the foundation of Ducati's success. The 900 Monster, introduced in 1993, was the first version of the stylish naked roadster. The brainchild of Miguel Angel Galluzzi, Il Monstro was a mishmash of other Ducati components: the engine was from the 900SS, the frame was an 851/888 part and the suspension and brakes were common to the 750SS. The whole was more than the sum of the parts however. Its exciting blend of performance and style made it a hit in European high streets, and a full capacity range soon followed. The latest fuel injected version of the Monster 900 offers improved performance and refinement.

Top speed:	208km/h (129mph)
Engine type:	904cc, a/c 90° V-twin, four-valve, SOHC desmodromic
Maximum power:	58kW (78bhp) at 7500rpm
Frame type:	steel-tube trellis
Tyre sizes:	front 120/70 17, rear 170/60 17
Final drive:	chain
Gearbox:	six-speed
Weight:	189kg (417lb)

Ducati Monster S4

By 2000, the 900 Monster was suffering attacks from several rival models, all with stronger powerplants. Cagiva's Raptor 650 and 1000 in particular were potent threats to the air-cooled Monster range.

So Ducati launched a new Monster, based around the engine and chassis from the ST4 sports-tourer. A re-tuned 916 engine gave the S4 the power it needed to take on its rivals, while a strong chassis with typical Ducati handling gave the S4 accomplished track handling.

The trademark Monster styling remained, only slightly marred by the large water radiator slung below the steering head, and many detail changes have tidied up the normally enclosed 916 engine.

New, higher-specification suspension units were also fitted. Fully adjustable Showa 43mm (1.7in) upside-down front forks and Sachs rear shock gave the new flagship Monster the sort of first-class damping and springing typical of a luxury Italian sports machine. The Brembo front brakes are common to the other Monsters, but are very effective on this faster machine.

While the new Monster S4 retains the same basic styling of the classic Monster range, there are several detail cosmetic changes. A neat headlight flyscreen offers little practical wind protection, but looks very stylish. Lightweight carbon-fibre

parts abound, including exhaust heat shields, sidepanels, mudguard and timing belt covers.

On the road, the S4 offers much more satisfying performance than the air-cooled 900. The engine is flexible and strong throughout the rev range, combining the muscular mid-range of the air-cooled engines with prodigious top-end power. The sports suspension gives a firm ride, which can be choppy over poor road surfaces, but is ideal on smooth racetracks. The S4 matches its competitors on styling and handling, although its 916cc engine just falls short of Cagiva's Raptor 1000 unit.

Top speed:	233km/h (145mph)
Engine type:	916cc, l/c 90° V-twin, eight-valve, DOHC desmodromic
Maximum power:	75kW (101bhp) at 8750rpm
Frame type:	steel-tube trellis
Tyre sizes:	front 120/70 17, rear 180/55 17
Final drive:	chain
Gearbox:	six-speed
Weight:	193kg (423lb)

Ducati 900SS

Ducati's 900SS is one of the firm's longest running models, and one of its most successful. Originally developed as an 860cc version of the bevel-drive 750SS, the first 900SS appeared in 1975, and was instantly popular. The early bike's basic principles of low weight, narrow chassis and sporting performance have stayed true to the latest version of the 900SS, first launched in 1998.

This 900SS uses the 904cc belt-drive engine common to all Ducati's current air-cooled 900s, including the Monster and the MH900. Single overhead camshaft desmo heads have two valves per cylinder, and the 900SS gained a fuel-injection system in 1998. While not very powerful compared with more modern Japanese designs, the 900SS motor provides very satisfying performance, the strong low-down torque delivery firing the rider out of bends like a slingshot, and the carburation is flawless throughout the rev range, right up to the redline.

The chassis, too, is a capable performer, despite its rather dated appearance. The welded steel-tube trellis frame is very stiff and light, while a simple cantilever rear monoshock and upside-down front forks give compliant, accomplished handling and good ground clearance. The low all-up weight of 188kg (414lb) and narrow dimensions help here too.

The most recent 1998 redesign was the responsibility of Ducati's design chief, Pierre Terblanche. The new full fairing gave more modern looks than the

previous design, and in addition a host of chassis modifications improved handling, although weight did increase slightly. New Brembo brakes and Showa forks came from the ST2 design, and a longer rear shock further improved the handling of this bike.

The engine was also overhauled in 1998, with new flywheel, different camshafts and modified pistons and cylinders, as well as the Weber-Marelli fuel-injection system. The fuel-injection allowed cleaner, more efficient running, while also increasing power.

Top speed:	225km/h (140mph)
Engine type:	904cc, a/c 90° V-twin, four-valve, SOHC desmodromic
Maximum power:	60kW (80bhp) at 7500rpm
Frame type:	steel-tube trellis
Tyre sizes:	front 120/70 17, rear 170/60 17
Final drive:	chain
Gearbox:	six-speed
Weight:	188kg (414lb)

Ducati 900SS FE

The FE stands for 'Final Edition', and the 900SS FE was a last special production run of the old carburettor-equipped SS before it was replaced in 1998. Based around the 900SS Superlight, the FE had special cosmetics, a tuned engine, and elegant chassis changes. The special silver single-seat bodywork was wrapped around a modified engine, with race-style high-level exhaust pipes. The front brakes have cast-iron racing discs and the black wheels are lightweight. A carbon-fibre clock surround, chainguard, mudguard and body panels complete the high spec. The FE's performance was only slightly improved over the standard bike, and it was really intended as a special celebration of the old model. Only 800 were produced.

Top speed:	225km/h (140mph)
Engine type:	904cc, a/c 90° V-twin, four-valve, SOHC desmodromic
Maximum power:	56kW (75bhp) at 7000rpm
Frame type:	steel-tube trellis
Tyre sizes:	front 120/70 17, rear 170/60 17
Final drive:	chain
Gearbox:	six-speed
Weight:	185kg (407lb)

Ducati MH 900

First seen at the 1998 Munich Intermot show, the MH900e was shown as a concept machine. Designed by Ducati designer Pierre Terblanche as a tribute to legendary racer Mike Hailwood and the Ducati machines of the 1970s, the MH900 has a unique style. Described by Ducati as 'neo-classical', it combines the elegant lines of the 900SS engine with traditional Ducati design motifs, and a healthy dose of modern influences. From the tiny front headlight through the red trellis frame and tubular single-sided swingarm, the MH900 looks like nothing else, save, perhaps, one of the 1970s machines which inspired it. Public feedback eventually persuaded Ducati to produce a limited run of 2000 MH900s, sold over the Internet.

Top speed:	225km/h (140mph)
Engine type:	904cc, a/c 90° V-twin, four-valve, SOHC desmodromic
Maximum power:	56kW (65bhp) at 8000rpm
Frame type:	steel-tube trellis
Tyre sizes:	front 120/65 17, rear 170/60 17
Final drive:	chain
Gearbox:	six-speed
Weight:	186kg (410lb)

Ducati 916 Biposto

Ducati's seminal sportsbike of the 1990s, the 916 is one of the truly great automotive designs. Unveiled to a stunned world in 1993, the 916 looked and went like no other machine around.

The 916 was a development of the firm's Desmoquattro superbikes, the 851 and 888. The engine was a similar 90° liquid-cooled V-twin with two camshafts and four desmodromic valves per cylinder. The desmodromic valve system – long favoured by Ducati – uses two rocker arms on each valve to positively close as well as open the poppet valves.

The four camshafts are driven by tough Kevlar toothed belts, and an advanced Weber-Marelli fuel-injection system provides fuel/air mix through large throttle bodies.

But it was the beauty of the design that impressed most. From the narrow twin slit headlamps, back across the flat-topped tank to the curvaceous seat unit, twin underseat silencers and single-sided swingarm, every inch of the 916 is innovative and gorgeous.

The 916 has the chassis credentials to back up its exotic looks. The steel-tube trellis frame is a development of the 888s, and has stiffness and lightweight which belies its low-tech appearance. High-specification racing suspension by Japanese firm Showa gave firm, precise track handling.

On the road, the 916 took sport riding to new levels. Although it did not have the high horsepower and light weight of Honda's CBR900RR FireBlade – the sportsbike king at the time – the 916's combination of superb handling, strong braking and incredibly torquey bottom-end and mid-range power made it an exhilarating ride.

However, it was on the track where the 916's fortune was really made. Together with the SPS and later 996 versions of the bike, it won four WSB titles between 1994 and 1999 with Carl Fogarty, as well as the 1996 championship with Troy Corser and the 2001 championship with Troy Bayliss.

Top speed:	261km/h (162mph)
Engine type:	916cc, l/c 90° V-twin, eight-valve, DOHC desmodromic
Maximum power:	78kW (105bhp) at 9000rpm
Frame type:	steel-tube trellis
Tyre sizes:	front 120/70 17, rear 190/50 17
Final drive:	chain
Gearbox:	six-speed
Weight:	203kg (448lb)

Ducati 916 SPS

The 916 was made available in SP (Sport Production) form between 1994 and 1996, with higher-specification engine internals, increased peak power and Öhlins suspension units. But for 1997, a more radical revamped SP Special was released. This machine was marked out by its increased capacity – the cylinders were bored out to 98mm (3.9in), 4mm (0.8in) more than the standard 916cc motor. The crankcases were altered and strengthened, larger valves and racing camshafts were fitted and a large-bore exhaust system helped boost peak power. This SPS is an amazing performer, particularly on the track, where its stiff frame, superb suspension and strong engine are allowed to shine.

Top speed:	280km/h (175mph)
Engine type:	996cc, l/c 90° V-twin, eight-valve, DOHC desmodromic
Maximum power:	92kW (123bhp) at 9800rpm
Frame type:	steel-tube trellis
Tyre sizes:	front 120/70 17, rear 190/50 17
Final drive:	chain
Gearbox:	six-speed
Weight:	190kg (418lb)

Ducati 996 Foggy Replica

The production of the original Foggy Replica 916 SPS was partly a marketing decision and partly a result of racing necessity. Ducati wanted to modify the frame of the 1998 World Superbike 916 SPS race bike, but homologation rules required a bike with this revised frame to be sold to the public. The factory therefore produced a limited run of 200 bikes with the slightly modified frame, and these were sold in Britain as Fogarty Replica machines, honouring English rider Carl Fogarty who won four WSB titles with Ducati. The new frame allowed a larger volume airbox, increasing power on the race bike. The road version wore race-replica stickers, an exotic titanium exhaust system, racing seat and lightweight Marchesini wheels.

Top speed:	280km/h (175mph)
Engine type:	996cc, l/c 90° V-twin, eight-valve, DOHC desmodromic
Maximum power:	93kE (124bhp) at 9800rpm
Frame type:	steel-tube trellis
Tyre sizes:	front 120/70 17, rear 190/50 17
Final drive:	chain
Gearbox:	six-speed
Weight:	187kg (412lb)

Ducati ST4

Ducati had launched its first sports touring machine, the ST2, in 1996, and although it was a success in many markets, it was also criticized for its lack of top-end power. So for 1998, Ducati expanded its sports touring range with a new ST4, while keeping the ST2 in production as a cheaper option.

The ST4 was basically an ST2 chassis and bodywork with a 916cc eight-valve desmodromic engine fitted. That engine installation was straightforward, although the front cylinder head was modified from the standard 916 Biposto design in order to fit the motor into the ST2 frame. The exhaust camshaft was moved down in the head by 10mm (0.3in), allowing the larger engine to fit.

The same steel-tube trellis frame, Showa upside-down front forks and Showa rear shock as the ST2 give the ST4 firm handling, although the more powerful engine places heavier stresses upon it.

For 2000, the ST4 was modified with several uprated parts. A wider rear wheel took a larger 180-section tyre, and the brakes and dash were uprated over the ST2 parts. A new sidestand design replaced the previous flip-up design and there were some detail engine changes, mostly to improve reliability.

On the road, the ST4 makes a capable sports tourer, although it is not as effective as Honda's VFR800. The engine is very strong, allowing all-day high-speed cruising,

and the 21-litre (4.6 gal) fuel tank gives a decent 320km (200 mile) range. Sporty handling makes short work of twisty back roads, while the strong Brembo brakes and sharp steering are even useful on the track.

Living with a Ducati ST4 is very easy – the dash has a comprehensive set of instruments, including an LCD screen with a clock and fuel gauge. The fairing provides decent weather protection, and the optional factory hard luggage fit well. The exhausts can also be moved up when the panniers are removed, increasing ground clearance.

Top speed:	244km/h (152mph)
Engine type:	916cc, l/c 90° V-twin, eight-valve, DOHC desmodromic
Maximum power:	80kW (107bhp) at 9000rpm
Frame type:	steel-tube trellis
Tyre sizes:	front 120/70 17, rear 180/55 17
Final drive:	chain
Gearbox:	six-speed
Weight:	215kg (474lb)

Ducati ST4S

Introduced in 2001, this sporting version of the ST4 has uprated suspension, chassis and engine components, and offers a much more dynamic package. The 916 engine of the ST4 is replaced with a larger-capacity 996 engine, a variant of the 996 superbike engine. Different valve timing and lift and revised fuel-injection give the ST4S engine a broad spread of power – peak torque of 72ft lb occurs at 7000rpm, and there is 60ft lb available at just 4000rpm. This strong bottom-end performance allows fast, easy progress, even with a pillion and loaded hard luggage. The enhanced chassis features uprated suspension and lighter wheels to improve dynamic performance. Stickier tyres supply extra grip to match the engine's power.

Top speed:	259km/h (161mph)
Engine type:	996cc, l/c 90° V-twin, eight-valve, DOHC desmodromic
Maximum power:	87kW (117bhp) at 8750rpm
Frame type:	steel-tube trellis
Tyre sizes:	front 120/70 17, rear 180/55 17
Final drive:	chain
Gearbox:	six-speed
Weight:	212kg (467lb)

Ducati ST2

Ducati's first attempt at a modern sports touring machine was introduced in late 1996. It used an enlarged version of the 1993 907ie 904cc engine, which was bored out to 944cc. This two-valve, SOHC desmodromic engine sits between the air-cooled SS and the four-valve liquid-cooled superbike engines in terms of power and performance. The revised engine was fitted into a relatively well-appointed chassis. The company's trademark steel-tube trellis frame is used, this time a variant of the Monster frame, itself developed from the 888 superbike design. Upside-down Showa front forks and Brembo brakes were lifted from the 916 sportsbike, and the rear monoshock suspension developed from the 916 but with double-sided steel swingarm.

Top speed:	220km/h (137mph)
Engine type:	944cc, l/c 90° V-twin, four-valve, SOHC
Maximum power:	62kW (83bhp) at 8500rpm
Frame type:	steel-tube trellis
Tyre sizes:	front 120/70 17, rear 180/55 17
Final drive:	chain
Gearbox:	six-speed
Weight:	209kg (460lb)

Ducati 996 Biposto

By 1998, the 916 was assailed by litre V-twins from several manufacturers, including Suzuki's TL1000R and Aprilia's RSV Mille, both more powerful than the 916.

Luckily for Ducati, it had already prepared a larger engine, in the shape of the 996cc engine used in the 916SPS. By the end of 1998, Ducati had released the 996 Biposto, an updated 916 with a 996cc engine. The 996 Biposto engine incorporated some features from the 916 design, and some from the SPS motor, including the pistons and crankcases. Other detail engine modifications included an updated fuel-injection system and more powerful alternator.

The 996 chassis was not dramatically changed from the 916 – there was little wrong with the old bike's handling. Nevertheless, new brakes from Brembo gave even better stopping performance, and other minor chassis modifications refined the handling and cut weight over the 916 by 5kg (11lb).

On the road, the 996 was much stronger than the 916, although it had less top-end power than the race-tuned 916SPS. And while the Aprilia RSV Mille and Suzuki's TL1000R still offered stronger engine performance, neither offered the mix of styling and track composure to match the Ducati.

For 2001, the last year of 996 production, Ducati offered three different versions.

The base 996 was similar to the 2000 bike, but with an Öhlins rear shock. A new 996 S was introduced, which had the 92kW (123bhp) 996SPS engine, Öhlins shock and Showa forks.

But the most interesting machine was the limited edition 996R, which featured the new Testastretta 'narrow head' engine. Produced to homologate the Testastretta engine for racing, the 996R was a £17,000 special. Fitted with full Öhlins suspension, carbon-fibre bodywork and the 101kW (135bhp) 998cc Testastretta engine, the 996R was the bike on which Troy Bayliss won his 2001 World Superbike title.

Top speed:	266km/h (165mph)
Engine type:	996cc, l/c 90° V-twin, eight-valve, DOHC desmodromic
Maximum power:	84kW (113bhp) at 8500rpm
Frame type:	steel-tube trellis
Tyre sizes:	front 120/70 17, rear 190/50 17
Final drive:	chain
Gearbox:	six-speed
Weight:	198kg (437lb)

Ducati 996 SPS

When Ducati fitted its 996cc engine to the base 996 model, it cancelled out most of the 916SPS's performance advantage. So when the 996SPS appeared towards the end of 1998, it was less impressive compared to the base bike than previously. Although the 92kW (123bhp) SPS engine still produced more power than the 84kW (113bhp) 996, Ducati had to make further chassis improvements to keep the SPS in its exalted position – and justify the high price. These mods included an Öhlins rear shock and lightweight five-spoke Marchesini wheels. And although the 1999 996SPS wore Showa forks, the 2000 model was uprated with exotic Öhlins fully adjustable forks, complete with titanium nitride coated stanchions.

Top speed:	280km/h (175mph)
Engine type:	996cc, l/c 90° V-twin, eight-valve, DOHC desmodromic
Maximum power:	92kW (123bhp) at 9800rpm
Frame type:	steel-tube trellis
Tyre sizes:	front 120/70 17, rear 190/50 17
Final drive:	chain
Gearbox:	six-speed
Weight:	190kg (418lb)

Ducati 998 Biposto

The 998 Biposto is a base model, but only in relation to the incredibly exotic 998S and 998R models in Ducati's 2002 range. Built around the WSB championship-winning 998cc Testastretta engine, the 998 Biposto was designed to challenge roadbikes like Honda's SP-2 and Aprilia's RSV Mille. The 998 uses the first generation Testastretta engine, which has a bore and stroke of 100 x 63.5mm (3.9 x 2.5in), allowing it to rev higher and produce stronger peak power. The 998's chassis is similar to the previous 996, with a steel-tube trellis frame, Öhlins rear monoshock and Showa upside-down front forks. The revised bodywork is sleeker, and loses the large air intakes on the side.

Top speed:	274km/h (170mph)
Engine type:	998cc, l/c 90° V-twin, eight-valve, DOHC desmodromic
Maximum power:	92kW (123bhp) at 9500rpm
Frame type:	steel-tube trellis
Tyre sizes:	front 120/70 17, rear 190/50 17
Final drive:	chain
Gearbox:	six-speed
Weight:	198kg (436lb)

Ducati 998 R

The 2002 model year brought yet another exotic, beautiful and incredibly powerful Ducati homologation racebike for the road. The 998R is powered by a road-going version of the second-generation Testastretta engine. This 999cc motor has a larger bore and shorter stroke (104 x 58.8mm/3.9 x 2.3in) than the 998S, which uses the previous Testastretta design.

The Testastretta (Italian for 'narrow head') design first appeared on the limited edition 996R race-replica of 2001. It was the first major redesign of the Desmoquattro engine since the 916 of 1994, with the aim of producing a new line of engines for future development. Ducati rearranged the desmodromic valve gear to bring the camshafts closer together and allow a narrower valve angle.

This narrower valve arrangement was essential to improve the combustion chamber shape for increased efficiency. The Testastretta also used a revised, short-stroke architecture, allowing higher revs and larger valves, while new stronger crankcases were designed to cope with the stresses of World Superbike racing. The latest version of Ducati's fuel-injection system uses a single 'shower'-type injector and 54mm (2.1in) throttle bodies.

This immensely strong engine is fitted to an equally impressive chassis. The frame is Ducati's trademark steel-tube trellis design, which offers excellent stiffness without excessive weight. The single-sided rear swingarm is heavier than a conventional

double-sided design, but has become iconic of the 916/996 range. Top-of-the-range Öhlins racing suspension front and rear is fully adjustable, and the forks are titanium nitride coated to reduce stiction. Racing four-pad Brembo brake calipers operate on floating discs bolted to graceful five-spoke Marchesini wheels. The beautiful fairing is slightly reshaped compared with the older 996, and is made of strong but light carbon-fibre.

Like the 996R of 2001, the 998R was a limited-edition production run, and many of these exotic thoroughbreds will end up on the racetrack.

Top speed:	280km/h (175mph)
Engine type:	999cc, l/c 90° V-twin, eight-valve, DOHC
Maximum power:	104kW (139bhp) at 10,000rpm
Frame type:	steel-tube trellis
Tyre sizes:	front 120/70 17, rear 190/50 17
Final drive:	chain
Gearbox:	six-speed
Weight:	183kg (404lb)

Ducati Multistrada

Launched as a concept machine at the 2001 Milan show, the Multistrada is a unique take on the dual-sport design from Ducati designer Pierre Terblanche. Echoing many of the design cues of Terblanche's earlier MH900 design, the Multistrada is a bold step, marrying roadbike chassis components with the tall seating position and narrow chassis of an off-road styled machine. The engine is an updated version of the firm's trademark air-cooled 90° V-twin, with two-valve desmodromic heads. The high-performance chassis includes a massive 190-section rear tyre, upside-down front forks and rear monoshock. The Multistrada is currently planned to go into production in early 2003.

Top speed:	225km/h (140mph) [estimate]
Engine type:	992cc, a/c 90° V-twin, four-valve, desmodromic valves
Maximum power:	not available
Frame type:	steel-tube trellis
Tyre sizes:	front 120/70 17, rear 190/50 17
Final drive:	chain
Gearbox:	six-speed
Weight:	195kg (430lb)

Gilera 600 Supersport

Gilera was important in road racing throughout the first half of the twentieth century, winning 44 Grand Prix titles before withdrawing from racing in 1957. More recently, it was better known for its small-capacity scooters. But with the Supersport 600, Gilera is aiming to return to the large-capacity sportsbike market. Unveiled in 2001, the Supersport 600 is intended to be in production for 2003. Gilera will use the Suzuki GSX-R600 engine, installed in its own high-specification chassis. An innovative titanium/aluminium frame uses aerospace glue to join the titanium steering head components to the aluminium beams, permitting light weight. A large central ram-air intake in the nose cone supplies cool air to the engine at high speeds.

Top speed:	266km/h (165mph)
Engine type:	599cc, l/c inline-four, 16-valve, DOHC
Maximum power:	89kW (120bhp) at 13,000rpm
Frame type:	aluminium/titanium bonded twin-spar
Tyre sizes:	front 120/70 17, rear 180/55 17
Final drive:	chain
Gearbox:	six-speed
Weight:	162kg (357lb)

Harley-Davidson 883 Sportster

The 883 Sportster is Harley's entry-level machine. A stripped-down, street-styled roadster, it has a narrow, lean look, unlike many of its larger siblings due to its simplicity. There is little to this bike apart from a narrow V-twin engine, a simple steel-tube frame and straightforward suspension components. The engine is a pushrod overhead valve design, first introduced in 1986. As standard, it is rather underpowered and restricted, but readily-available performance parts can easily increase power and torque. The chassis has limited sporting ability, at least in the traditional sense. It does have reasonable ground clearance though, and uprated suspension and brake components allow the owner to customize performance to suit.

Top speed:	177km/h (110mph)
Engine type:	883cc, a/c 45° V-twin, four-valve, OHV
Maximum power:	41kW (55bhp) at 5500rpm
Frame type:	steel-tube loop frame
Tyre sizes:	front 100/90 19, rear 130/90 16
Final drive:	chain
Gearbox:	five-speed
Weight:	235kg (518lb)

Harley-Davidson VRSCA V-Rod

Launched in 2001, the Harley Davidson V-Rod marked a radical departure for the American firm, in terms of styling, design and performance. It is based around a 86kW (115bhp) engine derived from the firm's VR1000 racebike. The engine – Harley's first production liquid-cooled V-twin – is thoroughly modern, with twin camshafts and four valves for each cylinder, fed by a powerful fuel-injection system. But it is the chassis which most impresses – a new, innovative take on the cruiser concept which at once looks modern and classic. The sinuous steel-tube frame is formed by pressurized water, while the body panels are made of brushed aluminium, and a ducted shroud guides cooling air to the hidden radiator.

Top speed:	217km/h (135mph)
Engine type:	1130cc, l/c 60° V-twin, eight-valve, DOHC
Maximum power:	86kW (115bhp) at 8250rpm
Frame type:	hydroformed steel-tube perimeter
Tyre sizes:	front 120/70 19, rear 180/55 18
Final drive:	belt
Gearbox:	five-speed
Weight:	270kg (595lb)

Harley-Davidson Road King

The Road King is Harley's interpretation of a touring machine. Fully equipped with hard pannier luggage, and a large detachable clear windshield upfront, this is a machine for long-distance cruising. Powered by the latest version of the firm's big twin motor, the Twin Cam 88, the 1449cc engine is fed by a 40mm (1.6in) CV carburettor, and exhausts its distinctive off-beat sound through crossover dual exhaust pipes. The chassis is typical Harley – solid, heavy and stable. Triple disc brakes provide decent stopping power, while the air-adjustable rear suspension allows the rider to adjust the ride for a passenger or full luggage load. It has dazzling chrome plate, fork shrouds and low-slung styling.

Top speed:	177km/h (110mph)
Engine type:	1449cc, a/c 45° V-twin, four-valve, OHV
Maximum power:	51kW (68bhp)
Frame type:	steel-tube backbone
Tyre sizes:	front 130/90 16, rear 130/90 16
Final drive:	belt
Gearbox:	five-speed
Weight:	332kg (732lb)

Harley-Davidson Dyna Glide

Harley's definition of 'Sport' differs from that of most other manufacturers. However, this Dyna Super Glide Sport offers a more performance-oriented Harley experience, and includes all the style and attitude of the firm's big twins. A 45º V-twin engine forms the design centrepiece, the 1450 Twin Cam design offering improved power, torque and refinement over the previous 1340cc engine it replaced in 1999. The rather vibey motor has rubber isolation mounts to prevent vibration reaching the chassis and rider. Harley's steel-tube cradle frame is a basic design, but bolted-on adjustable suspension and radial tyres provide better handling than the firm's less sophisticated models. Ground clearance is also much better.

Top speed:	177km/h (110mph)
Engine type:	1449cc, a/c 45° V-twin, four-valve, OHV
Maximum power:	51kW (68bhp)
Frame type:	steel-tube backbone
Tyre sizes:	front 100/90 19, rear 150/80 16
Final drive:	belt
Gearbox:	five-speed
Weight:	300kg (661lb)

Harley-Davidson Electra Glide

Combining inimitable Harley-Davidson cruiser styling with a premium tourer equipment package, the Electra Glide has long been Harley's flagship touring machine. From the fork-mounted fairing through the well-padded seat and large hard luggage system, it is built for two-up distance comfort. Extensive touring equipment such as a built-in stereo radio/cassette system, CB radio and intercom, and electronic cruise control make long journeys easier. The latest model uses a Twin Cam 88 engine, with twin camshafts operating overhead valves via pushrods, and electronic fuel-injection. Like all Harley cruisers, the Glide has strong low-down grunt, with rather weak top end power.

Top speed:	169km/h (105mph)
Engine type:	1449cc, a/c 45° V-twin, four-valve, OHV
Maximum power:	51kW (68bhp)
Frame type:	steel-tube backbone
Tyre sizes:	front 130/90 16, rear 130/90 16
Final drive:	belt
Gearbox:	five-speed
Weight:	385kg (849lb)

Harley-Davidson Fat Boy Twin Cam 88

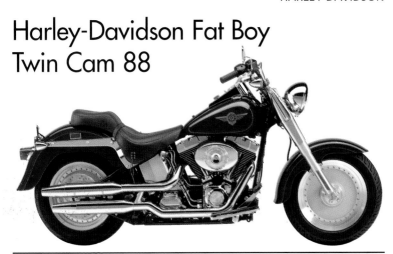

The Fat Boy is a stylish cruising variant of Harley-Davidson's Softail range, which uses a hidden rear suspension system to echo the hardtail systems of retro cruisers. The front suspension is also retro-styled, with large brushed alloy shrouds covering the sliders. The 2002 Fat Boy is fitted with the Twin Cam 88B balanced Harley engine. This motor – the first Harley engine with balance shafts – uses twin balancer shafts to cancel out the inherent vibration of the 45° V-twin motor. This balancing system allows more rigid mounting of the engine in the frame, improving stiffness. Available in either fuel-injected or carburetted versions, the 1450cc engine offers strong, smooth, low-down power, although it is weak at the top end.

Top speed:	177km/h (110mph)
Engine type:	1449cc, a/c 45° V-twin, four-valve, OHV
Maximum power:	51kW (68bhp)
Frame type:	steel-tube backbone
Tyre sizes:	front 90/90 16, rear 130/90 16
Final drive:	belt
Gearbox:	five-speed
Weight:	307kg (677lb)

Honda NC 30

Japan's home market had for many years a licence structure which restricted most riders to a 400cc or smaller machine. The result was a host of high-specification, scaled-down versions of larger sportsbikes, such as Honda's VFR400 NC30.

Designed as a 400cc version of the firm's legendary VFR750R RC30, the VFR400 has the distinctive single-sided swingarm, full race-style fairing and stiff, twin-spar extruded aluminium frame of the larger bike. Twin headlamps and a tiny pillion pad continue the race replica styling, and wide, multi-spoked aluminium wheels hold fat, sticky race tyres. Fully adjustable suspension and twin front brake discs complete the list of high-quality chassis components on display.

The engine also echoes the design of the RC30, although it uses a conventional camchain rather than the cam gear drive of the bigger bike. A compact, 90° V-4 design is narrower than an equivalent in-line four, allowing the neat dimensions of the VFR.

Tuned to produce a torquier power delivery rather than the peaky, revvy character normally associated with such small engines, the NC30 motor still manages a very respectable 48kW (65bhp) power output. That's enough for a top speed of around 217km/h (135mph), although many Japanese home market models were fitted with a 180km/h (112mph) speed restrictor.

Outside Japan, the VFR400 was eagerly welcomed by smaller road riders, particularly women, and 400cc Supersport class racers. It had the performance, styling and build quality to keep both road and race camps happy, and was a common sight on the podium at many race meetings worldwide.

The NC30 was discontinued in the early 1990s, replaced by the higher-spec RVF400R NC35. The NC35 used a similar engine and chassis, with upside-down front forks and a 43cm (17in) rear wheel, and was styled like the 750cc RC45 World Superbike racebike.

Top speed:	216km/h (135mph)
Engine type:	399cc, l/c 90° V-4, 16-valve, DOHC
Maximum power:	48kW (65bhp) at 9500rpm
Frame type:	aluminium twin-spar
Tyre sizes:	front 120/60 17, rear 150/60 18
Final drive:	chain
Gearbox:	six-speed
Weight:	164kg (362lb)

Honda CB500

The CB500 is Honda's take on the modern middleweight commuter bike, but with some differences. The engine is a conventional liquid-cooled parallel twin, with four-valve heads and balance shaft. The chassis is similarly unremarkable, being based around a simple steel-tube cradle frame, with a twin-shock rear swingarm and 37mm (1.5in) front forks holding rather narrow 43cm (17in) wheels and tyres. The CB500 was never designed as a race bike, so when Honda launched a one-make race series based round the model, it seemed a curious way to promote a simple roadster. But the lightly-modified bikes used in the series turned out to be surprisingly capable.

Top speed:	193km/h (120mph)
Engine type:	499cc, l/c parallel twin, eight-valve, DOHC
Maximum power:	42kW (56bhp) at 9500rpm
Frame type:	steel-tube cradle
Tyre sizes:	front 110/80 17, rear 130/80 17
Final drive:	chain
Gearbox:	six-speed
Weight:	173kg (381lb)

Honda CB500S

The CB500S appeared almost five years after the emergence of the base CB500. Honda had fitted a small, frame-mounted half-fairing and screen, which massively extended the CB500's practical range. The neat cowl, with built-in screen and even a small fairing pocket offers decent wind and weather protection on longer trips, as well as easing the strain on the rider at higher motorway cruising speeds. The fairing also integrates neatly with the base bike's radiator cowl. Apart from a small amount of extra weight over the front wheel, the CB500S has the same sharp handling and sprightly performance as the unfaired bike. Brembo disc brakes front and rear offer reliable, strong stopping power.

Top speed:	200km/h (125mph)
Engine type:	499cc, l/c parallel twin, eight-valve, DOHC
Maximum power:	42kW (56bhp) at 9500rpm
Frame type:	steel-tube cradle
Tyre sizes:	front 110/80 17, rear 130/80 17
Final drive:	chain
Gearbox:	six-speed
Weight:	177kg (390lb)

Honda Silver Wing

The European appetite for large-capacity scooters has been increasing since Suzuki's AN400 Burgman first appeared in 1999. Honda's Silver Wing is currently the biggest capacity scooter available, knocking Yamaha's 500cc T-Max off the top of the list. It uses a parallel-twin engine with four-valve heads and fuel-injection. Driving through a variable-belt automatic transmission, the liquid-cooled motor provides strong, usable power, managing 179km/h (112mph) on the speedometer. An advanced CBS linked braking system combines braking effort from front and rear levers for safer stopping. Conventional front forks and a twin-shock rear suspension system give handling that's closer to a conventional motorcycle.

Top speed:	179km/h (112mph)
Engine:	582cc , l/c eight-valve parallel twin, DOHC
Max power:	37kW (49.6bhp) at 7000rpm
Frame type:	steel-tube cradle
Tyre sizes:	front 120/80 14, rear 150/70 13
Final drive:	enclosed belt drive
Gearbox:	V-Matic automatic
Weight:	204kg (448lb)

Honda XLV600 Transalp

When it appeared in 1987, the Transalp was the latest in a line of fashionable 'dual sport' bikes from the big motorcycle manufacturers. Combining the best aspects of off-road machinery with a well-mannered road bike, they typically offer a softly tuned middleweight engine combined with trail-styled wheels and tyres and soft, long-travel suspension. The Transalp's engine has three-valve heads and liquid-cooling, and is tuned for flexibility rather than outright power. The soft suspension is unadjustable, and despite offering good comfort over rough surfaces, it is quickly overwhelmed by sporty riding. The Transalp's smart Euro-styling is distinctive, the small fairing and twin chromed silencers giving a compact, purposeful look.

Top speed:	176km/h (110mph)
Engine type:	583cc, l/c 52° V-twin, six-valve, SOHC
Maximum power:	37kW (50bhp) at 8000rpm
Frame type:	steel-tube cradle
Tyre sizes:	front 90/90 21, rear 120/90 17
Final drive:	chain
Gearbox:	five-speed
Weight:	196kg (431lb)

Honda CBR600F

Arguably the definitive middleweight Japanese sportsbike of the last decade or two, the CBR600 has been massively successful, both in terms of sales and on the racetrack, over its six major updates since being launched in 1987. From the first steel-framed model, with 63kW (85bhp) and 182kg (40lb) to the latest 81kW/170kg (109bhp/375lb) version, the CBR600 has always been the most usable of the sports 600 models.

This 2002 model, while retaining a family resemblance to its predecesors, is certainly the most advanced version yet. A light, compact, high-output four-cylinder engine fits snugly into a short, stiff aluminium twin-spar frame. High-specification suspension units front and rear give class-leading springing and damping performance, and wide, sticky radial sport tyres give amazing grip when cornering.

Smaller engines like the CBR600's are notoriously difficult to equip with fuel-injection, but the CBR's PGM-FI system is virtually flawless. An advanced CPU delivers finely metered fuel through a pair of 38mm (1.5in) dual-throat throttle bodies and also controls the ignition timing.

The four-piston front brake calipers are similar to the previous model's, but have been lightened with new aluminium pistons, and offer outstanding stopping performance. The fully adjustable suspension is comfortably soft on standard settings, but is easily altered to provide stiff, accurate racetrack performance.

But, like previous CBR600s, the latest model's success is down to more than its on-paper performance. It is also one of the most user-friendly bikes, and manages to be both comfortable and usable without compromising its sporting abilities.

The redesigned upper fairing, with twin 'fox-eye' headlamps and two sculpted air intakes, is aerodynamic enough for a 266km/h (165mph) top speed while giving the rider and pillion very acceptable wind protection. And while items like a key-mounted security immobilizer, pillion grabrail and a built-in mainstand do nothing for the CBR's sporting prowess, they make living with the CBR even easier.

Top speed:	266km/h (165mph)
Engine type:	599cc, l/c inline-four, 16 valve, DOHC
Maximum power:	81kW (109bhp) at 12,500rpm
Frame type:	twin-spar aluminium
Tyre sizes:	front 120/70 17, rear 180/55 17
Final drive:	chain
Gearbox:	six-speed
Weight:	170kg (375lb)

Honda CBR600FS

HONDA faced a tough dilemma with the 2001 update of its CBR600F all-rounder. The opposition had become much sportier and track-oriented, particularly Yamaha's R6 and the Suzuki GSX-R600K1. Honda engineers either had to move the CBR away from its practical everyman appeal, or find a compromise way to inject some much-needed sportiness. The CBR600F Sport, launched alongside the CBR600F, was the answer. The styling points to the track – a race-style stepped seat looks much sharper than the dual seat of the base CBR600F, and a smart black frame completes the cosmetic changes. No grabrail or centrestand saves 1kg (2.2lbs) in weight. The engine is modified for enhanced race tuning potential.

Top speed:	256km/h (160mph)
Engine type:	599cc, l/c inline-four, 16 valve, DOHC
Maximum power:	81kW (109bhp) at 12,500rpm
Frame type:	twin-spar aluminium
Tyre sizes:	front 120/70 17, rear 180/55 17
Final drive:	chain
Gearbox:	six-speed
Weight:	169kg (372lb)

Honda CB600 Hornet S

The major practical failing of Honda's original Hornet compared with its main competitors was the lack of any wind- or weather-protection on longer trips. Honda's answer was the Hornet 'S', launched two years after the base bike. A small bikini fairing gave the Hornet 'S' the long-distance capability it had lacked before. Year-round commuters and occasional tourers benefited from the higher top speeds and relaxed progress made possible by the screen, although many considered the naked bike the more stylish version. Honda also changed the front wheel size for this model year to a 43cm (17in) part. This allowed much wider tyre choice for the Hornet, and also applied to the unfaired bike from 2000 onwards.

Top speed:	232km/h (145mph)
Engine type:	600cc, l/c inline-four, 16-valve, DOHC
Maximum power:	70kW (94bhp) at 12,000rpm
Frame type:	steel-tube backbone
Tyre sizes:	front 120/70 17, rear 180/55 17
Final drive:	chain
Gearbox:	six-speed
Weight:	178kg (392lb)

Honda CB600F Hornet

The 'naked' 600cc sportster class was largely invented by Suzuki with its 600 Bandit in 1995. A combination of a sporty middleweight engine in a capable chassis was a huge sales success, and other firms soon launched their own naked 600s. Honda's answer was the CB600F Hornet, launched in 1998. Matching the styling of the Japan-only Hornet 250 with a retuned version of the CBR600F sportsbike engine, the Hornet 600 immediately looked like a winner.

The Hornet's inline-four engine produced almost 75kW (100bhp) – much more than the Bandit 600 – and the chassis looked simple and effective. A massive 180-section rear tyre came straight off the firm's FireBlade flagship sports machine, as did the unusual 40cm (16in) front wheel.

But the styling was the Hornet's ace card. A high-level single silencer dominated the rear end, together with a drilled heat shield and that fat rear tyre. The classic front end had just the basics – round headlight, chrome clocks, wide handlebars and a pair of stiff, conventional telescopic forks.

Riding the Hornet reinforces the image of a quick, fun machine. The 40cm (16in) front wheel and sharp steering geometry means quick handling, and the engine has plenty of top-end power for an exhilarating ride. It isn't all good news though: the twin-piston sliding caliper front brakes are indifferent, and the peaky engine needs to be revved hard to get the best from it.

But the Hornet's biggest problem was the competition. Yamaha's FZS600 Fazer, launched at the same time, had better brakes, a stronger engine and a half-fairing, for less money, and sold much better in the UK.

However, a one-make Hornet racing series in the UK increased interest in the bike, and provided lively, close racing.

For the 2000 model year, the Hornet's front wheel was replaced with a 43cm (17in) item, and there were minor updates to the styling and brakes.

Top speed:	224km/h (140mph)
Engine type:	600cc, l/c inline-four, 16-valve, DOHC
Maximum power:	70kW (94bhp) at 12,000rpm
Frame type:	steel-tube backbone
Tyre sizes:	front 120/70 17, rear 180/55 17
Final drive:	chain
Gearbox:	six-speed
Weight:	176kg (387lb)

Honda Deauville

The Deauville is a middleweight tourer/commuter with high equipment levels and practical design. Based around the NTV650 engine and chassis, the Deauville adds a touring fairing, complete with built-in panniers and a comfortable dual seat. There's an impressive range of official accessories, from larger panniers and top boxes to a CD/radio sound system. On the move, the liquid-cooled V-twin engine is not particularly powerful, but allows relaxed, economical progress. The soft suspension and shaft drive discourages sporty riding, but the Deauville is still commendably rapid across town or country roads. It is also popular with fleet users, and police, paramedic and courier Deauvilles are a common sight across Europe.

Top speed:	184km/h (115mph)
Engine type:	647cc, l/c 52° V-twin, six-valve, SOHC
Maximum power:	41kW (55bhp) at 7750rpm
Frame type:	twin-spar steel-tube
Tyre sizes:	front 120/70 17, rear 150/70 17
Final drive:	shaft
Gearbox:	five-speed
Weight:	228kg (502lb)

Honda Dominator

The Dominator, launched in 1988, is a middleweight 'dual sport' bike, with a torquey, air-cooled single-cylinder engine in a simple, trailbike chassis. Less capable off-road than its styling might suggest, the Dominator is best kept on the Tarmac, where its long-travel suspension and trail-type wheels and tyres work well on poorly surfaced roads. A compact half-fairing moulds into the fuel tank, giving smooth, aerodynamic looks, while a brushed aluminium bashplate under the frame and twin underseat 'shotgun' silencers complete the attractive styling. The engine is rather dated: its four-valve design is unchanged since 1988, and while the big single is strong low-down, it becomes breathless over 115km/h (70mph).

Top speed:	168km/h (105mph)
Engine type:	644cc, a/c single-cylinder, four-valve, SOHC
Maximum power:	31kW (41bhp) at 6000rpm
Frame type:	steel-tube cradle
Tyre sizes:	front 90/90 21, rear 120/90 17
Final drive:	chain
Gearbox:	five-speed
Weight:	167kg (367lb)

Honda SLR650

A budget, stripped-down version of the NX650 Dominator, the SLR650 is biased more towards the street part of the Dominator's street/dirt package. A 48cm (19in) front wheel replaces the Dominator's 53cm (21in) part, and the seat height is lower. The SLR is lighter than the Dominator, due to the lack of a top fairing, slightly improving acceleration. However, the SLR was built in Spain, and inconsistent quality control is below Honda's usual high quality. For a cheap, simple roadster though, the SLR's grunty, low-maintenance engine and soft suspension are perfectly acceptable. The trail-styled tyres give reasonable grip and disc brakes front and rear allow rapid stopping. The SLR650 was replaced in 1999 by the FX650 Vigor.

Top speed:	154km/h (96mph)
Engine type:	644cc, a/c single-cylinder, four-valve, SOHC
Maximum power:	24kW (32bhp) at 6150rpm
Frame type:	steel-tube single cradle
Tyre sizes:	front 100/90 19, rear 120/90 17
Final drive:	chain
Gearbox:	five-speed
Weight:	161kg (354lb)

Honda XLV650 Transalp

The XLV600 Transalp had managed 14 years in production with only slight modifications, but in 2001 Honda finally gave its middleweight 'dual sport' bike a makeover. The 583cc V-twin engine of the 600 was bored out to a larger 647cc version, and the bodywork was restyled with a sharp nosecone and headlamp. This echoed the firm's bigger bikes, especially the XL1000V Varadero. On the move, the update hasn't made a huge difference to the Transalp's performance. The engine is dated and underwhelming. The chassis offers safe, predictable if rather soft handling. The long-travel suspension gives a plush ride, and the dual seat is spacious and well-appointed, making the Transalp a decent light tourer.

Top speed:	184km/h (115mph)
Engine type:	647cc, l/c 52° V-twin, six-valve, SOHC
Maximum power:	40kW (53bhp) at 7500rpm
Frame type:	steel-tube cradle
Tyre sizes:	front 90/90 21, rear 120/90 17
Final drive:	chain
Gearbox:	five-speed
Weight:	191kg (420lb)

139

Honda CB Seven Fifty

When it first re-appeared in 1992, Honda's latest CB Seven Fifty was a rather different beast from its 1960s namesake. The original CB750 was the first real superbike, and revolutionized the biking world – a rather tall order for an air-cooled retro roadster in 1992.

The CB Seven Fifty's simple, unfaired chassis holds few surprises: a steel-tube cradle-type frame joins a twin-shock rear swingarm to the conventional telescopic front forks (based on the CBR600's items).

Twin front disc brakes wear dual-piston calipers, while the twin piggyback rear shocks and 41mm (1.6in) air-assisted forks offer comfortable, soft handling.

The engine is similarly anonymous, despite its 747cc capacity and double overhead camshaft design. It is based on the mid-1980s CBX750 design, its 16-valve head uses hydraulic tappets for low maintenance, while producing a lower output than the CBX, down to 53kW (71bhp) from 67kW (90bhp) and uses a five-speed gearbox, one less than the CBX. The CB's engine is willing enough at low to medium revs, but is less impressive at higher engine speeds: 145km/h (90mph) is its comfortable cruising limit. Windblast limits travelling much over 177km/h (110mph), and the CB struggles to its 193km/h (120mph) maximum speed.

Styling and build quality are the CB's strengths. A large round chrome headlamp

gives a classic look to the front end, and the deep paint finish and chrome megaphone exhaust impart a high-quality feel to the bike. A handy aluminium grabrail looks good as well as offering a secure grip for pillions and an easy-to-operate mainstand permits straightforward rear-end maintenance.

But for all its build quality and classic appeal, the CB Seven Fifty is a rather uninspiring machine, which would make a reasonable commuter or occasional Sunday cruising tool. Riders requiring long-legged touring ability or high-octane sporting thrills will probably look elsewhere.

Top speed:	193km/h (120mph)
Engine type:	747cc, a/c inline-four, 16-valve, DOHC
Maximum power:	53kW (71bhp) at 8500rpm
Frame type:	steel-tube double cradle
Tyre sizes:	front 120/70 17, rear 150/70 17
Final drive:	chain
Gearbox:	five-speed
Weight:	215kg (474lb)

Honda NR750

Perhaps the most exotic two-wheeled machine ever offered for sale, Honda's NR750 roadbike has achieved almost legendary status since it first appeared as a travelling marshal's bike at the 1990 Suzuka Eight Hour endurance race. Using a combination of racebike technology and early 1990s cutting-edge bike design, Honda created a V-4 oval-pistoned fuel-injected engine in a carbon-fibre clad supersports chassis, with styling and details that were a generation ahead of anything else available at the time.

The engine is perhaps the most impressive part of the NR750. The oval-piston design, first seen on Honda's NR500 Grand Prix bike, was an attempt to get V-8 power from the four cylinders allowed in GP competition. Honda's competitors were using two-strokes, and Soichiro Honda's fixation with four-stroke engines meant it was behind on power. An oval-pistoned V-4 has almost as much valve and piston area as an eight-cylinder motor, allowing similar power production to a V-8.

Each of the NR750's cylinders had two conrods, to prevent the oval piston rocking along its length, two spark plugs and eight valves: four inlet, four exhaust. An early version of Honda's PGM-FI fuel-injection managed the fuelling, and an incredibly complex eight-into-four-into-two-into-one-into-two titanium exhaust system emitted a beautiful sound.

The chassis, while extremely high-tech, is more conventional. Upside-down forks

and a single-sided rear swingarm were rare in 1992, but are common today.

The carbon-fibre bodywork set some styling cues for later bikes: the mirror-mounted indicators in the CBR1100 Super Blackbird, the louvres in the side fairing in the VFR750, and twin underseat exhausts have become a common sight on sportsbikes from Ducati's 916 to BMW's R1100S.

Other parts, such as the titanium-coated screen, head-up display and silver/carbon-fibre key are still the stuff of biking dreams.

Top speed:	257km/h (160mph)
Engine type:	748cc, l/c 90° V-4, 32-valve, DOHC, oval piston
Maximum power:	88kW (118bhp) at 14,000rpm
Frame type:	aluminium twin-spar
Tyre sizes:	front 130/70 16, rear 180/55 17
Final drive:	chain
Gearbox:	six-speed
Weight:	223kg (492lb)

Honda RC45

The entry rules for the World Superbike championship require the entered machinery to be based upon production bikes offered for sale to the public. This rule – intended to keep a link between the bikes on the track and the spectator's machines in the car park – has indirectly produced some of the finest road-going sportsbikes available, including Ducati's 916 and the RC45.

Based loosely around Honda's RVF750 endurance racebike, the RC45 was sold as an expensive, limited-edition racer for the roads, purely to enable its use in WSB racing.

To that end, the RC45 used only the finest-available technology and ancillary components. The single-seat frame is borrowed directly from racing machinery, and the V-4 engine, while based around the layout of the earlier RC30, is all-new. The camchain moved from the middle of the engine to the right-hand end, and a new short-stroke architecture of 72 x 46mm (2.8 x 1.8in) allowed higher revs and better peak power production. Titanium conrods and magnesium parts further reduced weight and improved reliability. Honda's PGM-FI fuel-injection system also made one of its first appearances on a roadbike.

Honda fitted a 40cm (16in) front wheel, although the race kit offered a 43cm (17in) option to allow better tyre choice. The fully adjustable suspension, supplied by Showa, was straight off the racetrack, and provided amazingly precise wheel control on track, as well as being very compliant on bumpy roads.

While the RC45 did its job – it won the WSB championship in 1997 with John Kocinski riding – it is a bit of a disappointment in terms of straight-line performance. In standard form, the engine isn't immensely powerful, and Honda's CBR900RR easily beat the RC45's performance – despite costing less than half as much.

However, many enthusiasts are still captivated by the design, handling and exotic reputation of the RC45, and its superb handling and balance make it one of the all-time great sportsbikes.

Top speed:	257km/h (160mph)
Engine type:	749cc, l/c 90° V-4, 16-valve, DOHC
Maximum power:	88kW (118bhp) at 12,000rpm
Frame type:	aluminium twin-spar
Tyre sizes:	front 130/70 16, rear 190/50 17
Final drive:	chain
Gearbox:	six-speed
Weight:	189kg (417lb)

Honda Africa Twin

Built in homage to the giant desert racers of the gruelling Paris–Dakar Rally, the Africa Twin is a huge, imposing trail-styled bike, powered by a rather softly tuned V-twin engine. First launched in 1990, the Africa Twin features fully-faired bodywork, including a large 23-litre (5 gal) fuel tank and a tall windscreen. A wide, long dual seat stretches back from the tank to a tough, aluminium grabrail/luggage rack, while a tough aluminium bashplate protects the bottom of the engine from flying rocks and impacts.

But, while the Africa Twin's styling points to off-road prowess, its detail design and performance suggests otherwise. The trail-styled knobbly tyres are designed for Tarmac use, and offer little grip on wet dirt or deep sand, while a close-fitting front mudguard quickly clogs with mud and debris. The plastic bodywork is easily damaged in the inevitable tumbles of off-road riding, and the 205kg (452lb) weight makes the XRV very hard to pick up after dropping it.

Kept on the road though, the Africa Twin works well as a touring bike and is also useful in town. There is plenty of weather protection from the fairing, and the large tank gives an extended range. The riding position is comfortable for extended two-up riding, and the rear rack is useful for carrying luggage. The seat is very high, however, and even average-height riders will struggle to touch the ground at traffic lights.

Although the 742cc liquid-cooled engine is rather dated and low on power, its

flexible delivery allows reasonable progress, and it is both reliable and economical. The long-travel suspension insulates the rider from uneven surfaces and while the twin-front and single rear brake discs are a trail-styled compromise, they work well enough in the context of the bike as a whole.

The XRV's instruments have some unusual additions: a large trip computer LCD display mounted above the conventional speedometer and tachometer is styled like Dakar racers' navigational displays, and incorporates a range of extra electronic timers and trip meters.

Top speed:	177km/h (110mph)
Engine type:	742cc, l/c 52° V-twin, six-valve, SOHC
Maximum power:	44kW (59bhp) at 7500rpm
Frame type:	steel-tube single cradle
Tyre sizes:	front 90/90 21, rear 140/80 17
Final drive:	chain
Gearbox:	five-speed
Weight:	205kg (452lb)

Honda VFR800

The VFR800 inherited its position as class leader in the sports-touring sector from its 750cc predecessor. Although its roots go back to the first VF750 of 1982, the latest VFR800 is one of the most accomplished and advanced motorcycles produced.

The V-4 engine at the heart of the VFR uses a VTEC variable valve system which alters the valve opening behaviour to give different power characteristics depending on engine speed. Below 7000rpm, only two of the four valves in each cylinder are opened by the camshafts. This two-valve layout gives superior torque and power production at low revs, where intake gas velocity is more important than large valve time-area values. But at higher revs (above 7000rpm) a computer-controlled valve pushes locking pins into place. These pins engage the remaining two valves in each cylinder, and the engine takes on the characteristics of a four-valve design. The extra valve time-area is perfectly suited to high-speed power production.

The VFR also features Honda's PGM-FI fuel-injection system, which boosts power, economy and clean-running, as well as a catalyzing element in the exhaust system to further reduce pollution.

The chassis combines sporting ability with touring practicality. A 'sport' version of the CBS linked brakes gives a more suitable blend of stopping power front and rear, while an optional ABS braking system provides extra security on unpredictable

road surfaces. Adjustable 43mm (1.7in) front forks and the single-sided monoshock rear suspension give superbly damped handling, and while the VFR is heavier than many sportsbikes, it disguises the extra mass well once on the move.

The broad dual seat is comfortable for many miles, even with a pillion, and the angular bodywork keeps the worst of the weather off. A generous 22-litre (4.8 gal) fuel tank, together with the efficient VTEC engine allows an impressive 322km (200 mile) range between refills. Optional accessories like hard luggage, heated grips and taller screens further enhance the VFR's touring ability.

Top speed:	256km/h (160mph)
Engine type:	782cc, l/c 90° V-4, 16-valve, DOHC
Maximum power:	80kW (107bhp) at 10,500rpm
Frame type:	aluminium twin-spar
Tyre sizes:	front 120/70 17, rear 180/55 17
Final drive:	chain
Gearbox:	six-speed
Weight:	218kg (480lb)

Honda Hornet 900

A larger version of the CB600F Hornet was predicted almost as soon as the smaller bike first appeared. But it took Honda until 2002 to finally launch the CB900F Hornet. Visually almost identical to the 600 Hornet, the 900 follows the tried and tested path of the smaller bike, using an older sportsbike engine in a cheap, simple steel-tube frame with off-the shelf chassis components.

The major visual difference is the exhaust system: the 900 has two underseat silencers with the header pipes tucked gracefully away beneath the engine, rising up through a hole in the swingarm. This centre-up design is shared with the 2002-model VFR800 VTEC, and lends a clean, uncluttered air to the Hornet's tail unit.

The Hornet 900's engine is a version of the 1998 FireBlade's powerplant which has been retuned for lower peak power and stronger low-down power. Valve timing and lift has been altered, and the compression ratio is lowered from 11.1:1 to 10.8:1, thanks to reshaped combustion chambers. The biggest change is in the intake system, where the FireBlade's carburettors have been replaced by 36mm (1.4in) fuel-injection throttle bodies. This PGM-FI system gives smooth power delivery and improved fuel economy, but its main function is to reduce exhaust emissions to comply with future legislation.

The steel-tube spine frame uses a similar design to the Hornet 600, but the square-section tubing uses thicker walls, up from 1.6mm (0.06in) to 2.3mm

(o.90in), and the steering head has been strengthened. In addition, the suspension and brakes are also upgraded compared with the smaller Hornet. Thicker, stiffer 43mm (1.7in) forks replace the 600's 41mm (1.6in) items, and the Hornet 900's front brakes use four-piston calipers, again borrowed from the earlier CBR900RR FireBlade.

The 900 doesn't have a fairing option, so is best kept away from motorways and long trips. But around town, and on twisty country roads, its compact dimensions, fast steering and torquey power delivery provide satisfying performance

Top speed:	232km/h (145mph)
Engine type:	919cc, l/c inline-four, 16-valve, DOHC
Maximum power:	81kW (109bhp) at 9000rpm
Frame type:	steel-tube spine
Tyre sizes:	front 120/70 17, rear 180/55 17
Final drive:	chain
Gearbox:	six-speed
Weight:	194kg (427lb)

Honda CBR900RR Fireblade

The FireBlade is arguably the first modern Superbike for the road. First launched in 1992, it soon became clear that the 'Blade was massively ahead of its competition in the litre-class sportsbike market. With a dry weight 24kg (53lb) lighter than its closest competitor, Yamaha's FZR1000 EXUP, the 185kg (407lb) CBR was the first bike designed to give control through lighter weight rather than brute power, and was extremely successful. The first-generation motor was an 893cc item, producing 91kW (122bhp), and the original FireBlade wore a then-unfashionable 40cm (16in) front wheel.

The FireBlade went through five generation changes before the CBR954RR version pictured here. The latest 954cc big-bore motor has gained Honda's PGM-FI fuel-injection system as well as a high-tech titanium exhaust valve, designed to improve mid-range torque by varying the characteristics of the exhaust system. The 40cm (16in) front wheel has gone, replaced by a 43cm (17in) item, and the front forks are an upside-down design, for reduced unsprung weight and improved stiffness. The rear swingarm is a 'works'-fabricated aluminium design, which is massively stiff.

What isn't so obvious is the weight loss. Despite producing 113kW (151bhp) at the crankshaft, the 2002 FireBlade weighs in at just 168kg (370lb) – lighter than most 600cc sportsbikes, including Honda's own CBR600F. It is also extremely compact, making it feel incredibly manageable and user-friendly both on the road and during track riding.

The market has moved on since 1992, and first Yamaha's R1 in 1998 then Suzuki's GSX-R1000 in 2001 have raised the stakes in the litre-class. The FireBlade has less power than both these bikes, but is lighter, giving it an edge in track handling, and has a strong blend of roadbike usability, excellent build quality and refined design.

However, it is not just in terms of performance hardware that the latest FireBlade excels. The tail lights use high-technology LEDs instead of conventional bulbs, and the all-electronic dash includes a fuel consumption meter, a tachometer, speedometer and clock.

Top speed:	280km/h (175mph)
Engine type:	954cc, l/c inline-four, 16 valve, DOHC
Maximum power:	113kW (151bhp) at 11,250rpm
Frame type:	twin-spar aluminium
Tyre sizes:	front 120/70 17, rear 190/50 17
Final drive:	chain
Gearbox:	six-speed
Weight:	168kg (370lb)

Honda VTR1000F Firestorm

After the success of Ducati's liquid-cooled eight-valve V-twin superbikes – the 748 and 916 – many Japanese firms were expected to launch competitor bikes. The Firestorm was Honda's first entry, appearing at the start of 1997.

The specification points to a high-tech sports machine. The Firestorm is built around a 996cc liquid-cooled 90° V-twin engine, with four valves per cylinder. Large 48mm (1.9in)CV carburettors, a massive airbox and twin-silencer exhaust system help provide smooth power delivery.

This engine is mounted in an advanced aluminium trellis spar design. The swingarm pivot is actually positioned below the end of the frame, at the back of the engine cases. This design saves weight and provides acceptable stiffness for road riding, although some racers have fitted reinforcing plates between the frame and the swingarm pivot to add stiffness for track use.

The running gear is standard mid-1990s Honda sports fare. The 41mm (1.6in) front forks are adjustable for spring preload and rebound damping, as is the gas-charged rear shock, while the Nissin four-piston front brake calipers are borrowed from the firm's CBR900RR FireBlade.

While the Firestorm is well-equipped, it offers a softer sports experience than something like Ducati's 916. The suspension is designed more for the road than the

track, and while the engine is strong, it has a softer edge than some more committed sports machines.

The Firestorm isn't excessively heavy at 192kg (422lb), but still compares badly with four-cylinder sportsbikes. Honda's FireBlade has always been lighter – the 2002 model is 24kg (53lb) lighter than the Firestorm. But kept in a sports touring role, the Firestorm is still satisfying, the low-down torque of the V-twin engine making for relaxed progress, and the neat half-fairing keeping the wind off at motorway speeds.

Top speed:	272km/h (170mph)
Engine type:	996cc, l/c 90° V-twin, eight-valve, DOHC
Maximum power:	82kW (110bhp) at 9000rpm
Frame type:	aluminium trellis twin-spar
Tyre sizes:	front 120/70 17, rear 180/55 17
Final drive:	chain
Gearbox:	six-speed
Weight:	192kg (422lb)

Honda VTR1000 SP-2

While Honda's VTR1000 Firestorm was a success on the road, it didn't have (and wasn't intended to have) the track ability required for Honda to beat Ducati in the world of racing. Ducati's 916 and 996 were dominating World Superbike, and Honda's V-4 RC45 was ageing fast. Honda had already decided to build a racing V-twin to beat Ducati at its own game.

The result, launched in 2000, was the VTR1000 SP-1. The 999cc V-twin engine owed little to the Firestorm's design, and featured an oversquare bore and stroke achitecture of 100 x 63.6mm (3.9 x 2.5in). An all-new PGM-FI fuel-injection system replaced the carburettors of the older bike, and the four camshafts were driven by accurate gear drive, rather than less-precise chains.

But it was the chassis which received most attention. Honda's racing division, HRC, provided the know-how to develop a new ultra-rigid aluminium twin-spar frame, using the engine as an extra load-bearing member within the frame. The frame also incorporates a cunning air inlet design: the distinctive front ram-air scoop between the fox-eye headlights runs straight through the cast aluminium steering head. This provides a direct path into the airbox for high-pressure air from the front fairing when the VTR is travelling at high racing speeds.

Showa fully adjustable suspension was among the highest quality fitted to any road bike, and four-piston Nissin calipers with large 320mm (12.6in) discs provided

ample stopping power, although Honda freely admitted it expected most racers to replace them with higher-spec racing parts.

The Honda SP-1 won the 2000 World Superbike championship first season out, with Colin Edwards riding, but Ducati retook the title in 2001. Honda therefore took the lessons learned in the SP-1's first season, producing the SP-2 for 2002. A stronger, more rigid frame and swingarm are identical to the WSB race bike parts, and a host of engine modifications boosted peak power by 3kW (4bhp), and cut weight by 5kg (11lb).

Top speed:	274km/h (170mph)
Engine type:	999cc, l/c 90° V-twin, eight-valve, DOHC
Maximum power:	99kW (133bhp) at 10,000rpm
Frame type:	aluminium twin-spar
Tyre sizes:	front 120/70 17, rear 190/50 17
Final drive:	chain
Gearbox:	six-speed
Weight:	194kg (427lb)

Honda Varadero

Honda's entry to the large-capacity trailbike sector is much more road-biased than many of its competitors. While the Varadero has the long-travel suspension, large fuel tank and tall seating position of a typical big traillie, it has more road-friendly aluminium wheels, with radial, tubeless tyres better suited to high-mileage use on Tarmac.

Honda didn't have to look too hard for an engine to fit the Varadero: the firm's VTR1000F Firestorm engine was narrow, powerful and torquey enough to make an ideal touring trailbike powerplant. Further re-tuning in the shape of smaller 42mm carbs gives even more bottom-end strength at the expense of top-end power. The VTR's gearbox also lost a gear, giving the Varadero a five-speed gearbox, more suitable for its broader spread of power.

From the rider's seat, the Varadero seems huge. The tall screen stretches out in front, and the large 25-litre (5.4 gal) fuel tank swoops down either side. Faired-in side-mount radiators allow a shorter wheelbase, but add even more width to the fairing.

The 'pivotless' steel frame uses the engine as a stressed member; the aluminium swingarm pivots directly in the engine cases. Suspension is only adjustable for rear spring preload, but the 43mm (1.7in) front forks and rear monoshock offer plush damping and plenty of travel to soak up the worst of road conditions. Honda's CBS linked brakes are standard equipment, linking the front and rear

braking systems through a series of linkages and control valves for improved braking control.

Equipped with hard luggage, the Varadero (improbably named after a Cuban seaside town) makes a comfortable, fast tourer. Two-up accommodation is spacious and comfortable. There is sufficient power for fast 160km/h (100mph) plus cruising speeds.

The Varadero's only touring flaw is excessive fuel consumption: ridden hard, the Varadero can return less than 10km/l (30mpg), despite its large fuel tank.

Top speed:	216km/h (135mph)
Engine type:	996cc, l/c 90° V-twin, eight-valve, DOHC
Maximum power:	71kW (95bhp) at 8000rpm
Frame type:	'pivotless' steel-tube cantilever
Tyre sizes:	front 110/80 19, rear 150/70 17
Final drive:	chain
Gearbox:	five-speed
Weight:	220kg (484lb)

Honda CBR 1000F

Before the CBR1100XX Super Blackbird appeared in 1996, the CBR1000F was Honda's fast sports tourer. When the CBR1000 first appeared in 1987, alongside its smaller 600cc sibling, it was one of the fastest, most accomplished machines available, and later versions had even better performance and handling.

A turbine-smooth inline-four cylinder engine provides good straight-line performance, up to and beyond 260km/h (160mph), while remaining impressively civil at more moderate speeds. An unremarkable, 16-valve inline-four design, its smoothness and flexibility are its trump cards, although it lacks outright top-end power compared to more recent large-capacity motors.

The chassis, while overweight and soft by modern standards, is very capable, offering extremely stable handling at motorway speeds. The relaxed steering geometry and large mass do mean that the big CBR steers rather slowly though, so it's not at its best on twisty back roads or race tracks.

The CBR10000F is suitable for high-speed two-up touring, helped by its all-enveloping bodywork. The broad screen guides wind round the rider, and a deeply-padded comfortable dual seat gives ample accommodation for rider and pillion.

The CBR1000 was the first Honda to feature the firm's Dual-CBS linked brakes. This system uses an arrangement of slave cylinders, linkages and valves to link the front

and rear brake circuits to provide improved stopping performance. Pulling the brake lever on the handlebars operates two of the three pistons on each front caliper, and one of the three pistons in the rear caliper. Pushing the foot brake pedal operates the remaining piston in the front calipers, and the two remaining pistons in the rear caliper. While the system works well, some advanced riders complain that it removes ultimate braking control from the rider.

The CBR1000 was discontinued in 1999, the Super Blackbird having largely replaced it at the top of Honda's fast sports touring range.

Top speed:	266km/h (165mph)
Engine type:	998cc, l/c inline-four, 16-valve, DOHC
Maximum power:	101kW (135bhp) at 9500rpm
Frame type:	steel-tube perimeter
Tyre sizes:	front 120/70 17, rear 170/60 17
Final drive:	chain
Gearbox:	six-speed
Weight:	235kg (518lb)

Honda Blackbird

Prior to the launch of Honda's Super Blackbird in 1996, the 'World's Fastest Production Bike' crown had long belonged to Kawasaki's heavyweight ZZ-R1100. But when the world's press first rode the new big-bore Honda at the Paul Ricard circuit in France, it became clear the Blackbird would live up to the high-speed reputation of the spyplane it took its name from, Lockheed's SR71 'Blackbird'.

The Blackbird used a 1137cc inline-four 16-valve engine, using many of the same design principles as the firm's smaller CBR900RR FireBlade. This allowed Honda to produce an extremely powerful engine that was much lighter and more compact.

The other part of the Honda's high-speed equation was its aerodynamic design. From the large front mudguard to the then-unusual stacked headlight design and back through the slippery fairing and sleek tail unit, the Blackbird was built to cut through the air with ease. The latest version of the bike, which first appeared in 1999, can reach speeds well over 270km/h (170mph). The 1999 update improved the Blackbird in a number of areas – PGM-FI fuel-injection replaced the old model's carburettors, correcting an annoying flat spot in the original bike's power delivery. The two intakes below the headlight were also fed into a sealed ram-air box, rather than simply cooling the oil radiator previously located there.

But the Blackbird's success has been down to more than just power and top speed. Honda managed to provide comfortable accommodation for two, and high levels of

equipment, turning the Blackbird into a highly accomplished, high-speed sports tourer. Despite a hefty dry weight of 224kg (493lb), the CBR's plush suspension and stable handling make it more capable on twisty roads than might be expected.

The Blackbird also features Honda's CBS linked brakes. A system of linked calipers and control valves means that pulling the front brake lever also operates the rear brake, and vice versa. The system is intended to give improved, controlled stopping, but has been criticized by experience riders for removing independent braking control over either end.

Top speed:	280km/h (175mph)
Engine type:	1137cc, l/c inline-four, 16-valve, DOHC
Maximum power:	113kW (152bhp) at 9500rpm
Frame type:	aluminium twin-spar
Tyre sizes:	front 120/70 17, rear 180/55 17
Final drive:	chain
Gearbox:	six-speed
Weight:	224kg (493lb)

Honda
X-Eleven

Honda's X-Eleven is a naked 'musclebike' based on the firm's superfast sports tourer, the CBR1100XX Super Blackbird. The styling is dominated both by the immense inline-four engine and the massive radiator shroud. This shroud, together with the instrument surround, guides some windblast past the rider at high speeds, without using a conventional fairing or screen. The shroud also pushes the front wheel down into the ground at higher speeds, like a sports car's front spoiler.

Both the engine and the chassis are based upon the Blackbird's, but with slight modifications. The engine has five gears, one less than the Blackbird, and one of the Blackbird's twin balance shafts has been removed to give a more 'raw' feel to the X-Eleven's engine. The aluminium twin-spar frame uses a 'centre pivot' design which allows controlled flex within the chassis. The well-damped suspension is also developed from the Blackbird.

On the road, the X-Eleven is dominated by its massive engine. The 100kW (134bhp) inline-four powerplant is re-tuned for less top-end power, without the pressurized ram-air intakes of the Blackbird, but is still immensely strong all through the rev range. It's easily strong enough to lift the front wheel off the throttle in first gear, and capable of 249km/h (150mph), though is totally civilized at more sedate speeds.

Honda chose to fit its CBS linked brakes to the X-Eleven, although they are not to every rider's taste. A complex, heavy system of hoses, valves and secondary master

cylinders link both front and rear brake circuits, with indifferent results. When the rider pulls the handlebar lever, two of the three pistons in each front brake caliper are operated, together with one piston in the rear caliper. When the foot brake pedal is pushed, the remaining piston in each front caliper and two pistons in the rear caliper are operated.

The X-Eleven was never a sales success, and the 2002 introduction of the lighter, cheaper Hornet 900 seemed to sound the final death knell for the quirky heavyweight.

Top speed:	249km/h (155mph)
Engine type:	1137cc, l/c inline-four, 16-valve, DOHC
Maximum power:	100kW (134bhp) at 9000rpm
Frame type:	aluminium twin-spar, 'centre pivot' system
Tyre sizes:	front 120/70 17, rear 180/55 17
Final drive:	chain
Gearbox:	five-speed
Weight:	222kg (489lb)

Honda
Pan European

H onda's ST1100 Pan European was first launched in 1989, and continued largely unchanged until 2002, when this 1261cc updated model was launched. The original Pan was a huge success in the heavy tourer market, its 1100cc V-4 engine and accomplished chassis winning acclaim from riders worldwide. But by 2002, it was starting to look dated in comparison with competition from bikes like Yamaha's FJR1300 and BMW's R1150RT. So Honda embarked on a ground-up revamp of the Pan.

The new bike, dubbed the STX1300 Pan European, retains the same transverse V-4 layout of the older bike, but has an all-new chassis and engine. An aluminium frame saves weight and adds stiffness compared with the older steel frame, and the large-capacity engine is packed with modern technology to produce even more torque and power.

Ceramic coated aluminium bores cut weight and friction inside the engine, while lasting longer than the old steel liners. New lightweight pistons further reduce friction, and the old bike's camshaft belt drive is replaced by a smaller, maintenance-free chain. This new cam drive, together with a repositioned alternator, makes the engine shorter and more compact.

New dual balancer shafts cut vibration from the already smooth motor, while a PGM-FI fuel-injection system replaces the ST1100's carbs.

A new lightweight aluminium swingarm further refines the rear monoshock suspension while the front end is fitted with stiff 45mm (1.8in) forks. Honda's Dual-CBS linked brake system is fitted to the new model, and optional anti-lock brakes are also available. Redesigned bodywork updates the Pan's looks while remaining true to the original bike's styling.

Honda offers a wide variety of optional accessories for the STX1300: owners can choose from a list that includes a large-capacity topbox, CD/radio sound system and heated grips. The stripdown picture above show the earlier ST1100 Pan European.

Top speed:	240km/h (150mph)
Engine type:	1261cc, l/c 90° V-twin, 16-valve, DOHC
Maximum power:	87kW (117bhp) at 8000rpm
Frame type:	extruded/cast aluminium diamond
Tyre sizes:	front 120/70 17, rear 170/60 17
Final drive:	shaft
Gearbox:	five-speed
Weight:	283kg (622.6lb)

Honda Valkyrie

In a market dominated by larger-than-life bike designs, the F6C Valkyrie really stands out. It uses the flat-six engine from the GL1500 Gold Wing, which first appeared in 1988. This is a very smooth design, with a belt-driven SOHC valvetrain, driving through a five-speed gearbox and shaft drive. Honda's engineers fitted sportsbike suspension and brakes. Upside-down 45mm (1.8in) front forks are massively stiff, and the twin front discs provide ample stopping power for such a heavy machine. Twin rear shocks have spring preload adjustment, and the steel frame provides a stiff, stable basis, giving surprisingly good handling. The Valkyrie steers easily, and corners superbly to the limits of its ground clearance.

Top speed:	200km/h (125mph)
Engine type:	1520cc, l/c flat-six, 12-valve, SOHC
Maximum power:	75kW (100bhp) at 6000rpm
Frame type:	steel-tube spine
Tyre sizes:	front 150/80 17, rear 180/70 16
Final drive:	shaft
Gearbox:	five-speed
Weight:	309kg (680lb)

Honda VTX 1800

The VTX1800 proves that one-upmanship is alive and well in the bike world. The biggest V-twin in production, the VTX motor is a truly outrageous piece of engineering. Its pistons measure 101mm (4in) across, larger than any other Honda piston. And while the peak power output isn't so impressive, the VTX manages a monstrous torque figure of 115lb ft at just 3000rpm. While the low-slung dragster styling of the VTX echoes older bikes, the big Honda is packed with high-tech features. Its liquid-cooled multi-valve engine is fed by an advanced fuel-injection system, and uses a compact dry-sump lubrication system. The brakes use a version of Honda's Dual-CBS linked system, and the front forks are 45mm (1.8in) upside-down items.

Top speed:	216km/h (135mph)
Engine type:	1795cc, l/c 52° V-twin, six-valve, SOHC
Maximum power:	71kW (95bhp) at 5000rpm
Frame type:	steel-tube cradle
Tyre sizes:	front 130/70 18, rear 180/70 16
Final drive:	shaft
Gearbox:	five-speed
Weight:	320kg (704lb)

Honda Gold Wing

The Gold Wing is one of the longest-running models still on the market: the original model was the GL1000, launched in 1975. The engine has since increased in size to this 1800cc model of 2001. The engine layout has also changed, from the original flat-four to a flat-six, and features Honda's PGM-FI fuel-injection system. The GL1800 is perhaps the ultimate touring machine, with an equipment list more like a luxury car. From the CD sound system, 147-litre (32 gal) luggage space and reverse gear to cruise control, heated grips and trip computer, the Gold Wing is simply the best-equipped bike available. Its chassis is based on a twin-spar aluminium frame, with 45mm (1.8in) front forks and CBS linked brakes.

Top speed:	225km/h (140mph)
Engine type:	1832cc, l/c flat six, 12-valve, SOHC
Maximum power:	87kW (117bhp) at 5500rpm
Frame type:	aluminium twin-spar
Tyre sizes:	front 130/70 18, rear 180/60 16
Final drive:	shaft
Gearbox:	five-speed
Weight:	363kg (799lb)

Husqvarna SM610

Originally Swedish, the Husqvarna company was taken over by Cagiva in 1986, and is now based at the Cagiva plant in Varese, Italy. The firm's latest machinery is built around a 576cc single-cylinder four-stroke engine. The SM610 Supermotard follows the familiar continental route of fitting lightweight 43cm (17in) wheels, large racing brake discs and sticky sports tyres to a low-geared, torquey off-road machine. The result is a quick, highly manoeuvrable bike, which enthusiasts claim is a match for conventional superbikes on tight, twisty mountain roads. Despite a comparatively low top speed, the SM610 has blistering acceleration, which with its light weight and high-quality suspension makes it exciting to ride.

Top speed:	169km/h (105mph)
Engine type:	576cc, l/c single-cylinder, four-valve, SOHC
Maximum power:	41kW (55bhp) at 6000rpm
Frame type:	steel-tube cradle
Tyre sizes:	front 120/70 17, rear 150/60 17
Final drive:	chain
Gearbox:	six-speed
Weight:	150kg (330lb)

Husqvarna TE610

The TE610 is Husqvarna's entry in the unlimited enduro bike class. Based around the firm's liquid-cooled single-cylinder 576cc engine, the TE shares many parts with the SM610 Supermotard and the TC570 motocross bike. The TE610 slots the 576cc motor into a conventional dirtbike cradle-type frame, with adjustable front forks and rear monoshock. Enduro-style lights and instruments make the TE road-legal, just about, although the small 9-litre (2 gal) fuel tank and narrow seat rule out any serious distance work. Like the SM610, many owners use the TE as a dual-purpose on/off road machine. A spare set of 68cm (17in) spoked wheels are quickly swapped for the enduro bike's knobblies.

Top speed:	169km/h (105mph)
Engine type:	576cc, l/c single-cylinder, four-valve, SOHC
Maximum power:	41kW (55bhp) at 6000rpm
Frame type:	steel-tube cradle
Tyre sizes:	front 90/90 21, rear 140/80 18
Final drive:	chain
Gearbox:	six-speed
Weight:	150kg (330lb)

Kawasaki ZXR400

Kawasaki's ZXR400 is a scaled-down version of the larger ZXR750 sportsbike, in looks and intent. A race styled twin headlight fairing is mounted on a stiff aluminium frame, with race-spec suspension and a high-performance inline-four cylinder engine. The engine is dated, but strong for its size. Like all 400cc engines, the ZXR needs to be revved to produce its best power, but a keen rider will reap the benefits of careful gear selection. A slick six-speed gearbox helps, as does the ZXR's light clutch. Ridden on track, the ZXR400's light-weight, accurate chassis and race-developed brakes allow extreme cornering at high speeds. The 41mm (1.6in) front forks and the rear shock are adjustable for preload and damping.

Top speed:	224km/h (140mph)
Engine type:	398cc, l/c inline-four, 16-valve, DOHC
Maximum power:	48kW (65bhp) at 13,000rpm
Frame type:	twin-spar aluminium
Tyre sizes:	front 120/60 17, rear 160/60 17
Final drive:	chain
Gearbox:	six-speed
Weight:	162kg (357lb)

Kawasaki ER-5

The ER-5 uses the well-proven parallel twin engine from the GPZ500S in a basic roadster chassis. Aimed at novices and commuters, rather than sports riders, the ER-5 nevertheless offers economical performance and sure-footed handling. The steel-tube cradle frame is stiff enough for the 37kW (50bhp) the re-tuned GPZ engine pumps out, and although the suspension is rather soft, the ER-5's light weight means it hasn't got too much work to do. That low mass helps the brakes too, although the single front disc and drum rear aren't the strongest stoppers on the market. The sculpted tank holds only 15 litres (3.5 gal), but the 498cc engine easily returns over 60mpg, giving an impressive range.

Top speed:	201km/h (125mph)
Engine type:	498cc, l/c parallel-twin, eight-valve, DOHC
Maximum power:	37kW (50bhp) at 9000rpm
Frame type:	steel-tube double cradle
Tyre sizes:	front 110/70 17, rear 130/70 17
Final drive:	chain
Gearbox:	six-speed
Weight:	179kg (395lb)

Kawasaki GPZ500

First launched in 1987, the GPZ500S was Kawasaki's attempt at a modern, lightweight sportsbike. Its parallel twin engine owes much to the GPZ900R of 1984: in many ways, it resembles half a GPZ900R engine. The chassis is dated, but is still capable of being hussled down a fast back road or round a track. The suspension is too soft to offer truly sporting performance, but the brakes work well if kept in good order, and the relaxed steering geometry means predictable handling. In 1994, the GPZ500 received a facelift. New bodywork gave a more up-to-date appearance, while 43cm (17in) wheels allowed modern rubber to be fitted. Wider 37mm (1.5in) front forks stiffened the chassis.

Top speed:	209km/h (130mph)
Engine type:	498cc, l/c parallel-twin, eight-valve, DOHC
Maximum power:	45kW (60bhp) at 10,000rpm
Frame type:	steel-tube double cradle
Tyre sizes:	front 110/70 17, rear 130/70 17
Final drive:	chain
Gearbox:	six-speed
Weight:	176kg (388lb)

Kawasaki KLE500

Kawasaki's KLE500 is a rather unusual design, loosely based around the 'dual sport' concept which mixes road and off-road design elements. A re-tuned parallel twin engine from the GPZ500S was fitted into a steel-tube frame with long-travel suspension, dirt-style spoked wheels, and a small top fairing. The single disc brakes and tyres front and rear are also off-road items. But the off-road styling is just that, and the KLE isn't really suitable for dirt use, where its weight, fragile bodywork and unsophisticated suspension count against it. It does make a useful commuter though; its economical, reliable engine gives dependable service, and the soft suspension tames typically bumpy city streets. The KLE was discontinued in 1998.

Top speed:	185km/h (115mph)
Engine type:	498cc, l/c parallel twin, eight-valve, DOHC
Maximum power:	37kW (50bhp) at 9000rpm
Frame type:	steel-tube cradle
Tyre sizes:	front 90/90 21, rear 130/80 17
Final drive:	chain
Gearbox:	six-speed
Weight:	178kg (392lb)

Kawasaki Zephyr 550

The Zephyr 550 was the smallest of the Zephyr range, and in some ways ahead of its time. Launched in 1991 as a stylish naked retro roadster, it occupied a niche later made very successful by Suzuki's Bandit. It used the air-cooled engine from the GPZ550, de-tuned for mid-range power, with minor cosmetic changes. The elderly engine was installed in a good-looking rolling chassis. A box-section aluminium twin-shock swingarm used sports-style eccentric chain adjusters, while a classically styled fuel tank and chrome-plated exhaust system rounded off the handsome design. The Zephyr's straight-line performance was disappointing though: the engine that produced 48kW (65bhp) in the GPZ550 was retuned to make just 37kW (49bhp).

Top speed:	185km/h (115mph)
Engine type:	553cc, a/c inline-four, eight-valve, DOHC
Maximum power:	37kW (49bhp) at 10,000rpm
Frame type:	steel-tube double cradle
Tyre sizes:	front 110/80 17, rear 140/70 18
Final drive:	chain
Gearbox:	six-speed
Weight:	179kg (395lb)

Kawasaki ZX-6R Ninja

Kawasaki's entry to the 600cc supersports class first appeared in 1995, relegating the elderly ZZ-R600 to a sport-touring role. The first F1 model set a reputation for strong engine performance, fine handling and usable road manners which following models have maintained.

There is nothing remarkable about the ZX-6R's design, although its high-spec aluminium frame was ahead of its competitors when launched – Yamaha's FZR600 and Honda's CBR600 both had steel frames in 1995.

A liquid-cooled 16-valve inline-four engine is unremarkable, but the Kawasaki engine was very strong, a ram-air system helping it produce an impressive 75kW (100bhp).

By 2001, the ZX-6R had been comprehensively updated, and was more than competitive in this intensely fought class. The basic design was the same, but numerous refinements had turned the ZX-6R into an accomplished, user-friendly sportsbike. The carburettor-equipped engine is still among the most powerful available, and cunning combustion chamber design has given it a strong, torquey bottom end.

The front and rear suspension units are of unassuming appearance, but are fully adjustable and perform well on road and track. Six-piston calipers are again unique in the class, but the ZX-6R's Tokico brakes are outclassed by the competition,

particularly the Sumitomo calipers on Yamaha's R6.

The ZX-6R's dry weight of 171kg (377lb) isn't the best in its class, but makes little difference to its performance except on track. However, a ZX-6R ridden by Australian Andrew Pitt won the 2001 World Supersport title, suggesting its track potential is more than sufficient.

On the road, the strong engine makes easy work of any traffic or road conditions, and the broad fairing gives impressive weather- and windblast protection.

Top speed:	257km/h (160mph)
Engine type:	599cc, l/c inline-four, 16-valve, DOHC
Maximum power:	83kW (111bhp) at 12,500rpm
Frame type:	twin-spar aluminium
Tyre sizes:	front 120/65 17, rear 180/55 17
Final drive:	chain
Gearbox:	six-speed
Weight:	171kg (377lb)

Kawasaki ZZR600

The ZZ-R600 is one of Kawasaki's most successful sports models. First introduced in 1990, along with its 1100cc sibling, the ZZ-R1100, the ZZ-R600 offered an extremely fast and powerful roadbike package. A strong inline-four liquid-cooled engine producing nearly 75kW (100bhp), aerodynamic bodywork and a power-boosting ram-air intake system all conspired to produce a top speed of well over 240km/h (150mph).

But it wasn't only the ZZ-R's top speed which made it so remarkable. Its advanced, stiff, lightweight aluminium twin-spar frame was unknown in the Japanese 600 class at the time, and it immediately marked the ZZ-R out as a high-quality product. Detail styling cues like the faired-in rear indicators and aerodynamic mirrors all suggested speed, although Kawasaki clearly hadn't forgotten about more mundane matters like chain oiling – a centrestand is tucked neatly away under the twin silencers.

The chassis is less sporting than the strong engine, but is capable of handling most road-based sports riding. Its four-piston front brake calipers give strong, progressive stopping power. But the suspension, updated in 1995, is rather soft, and compromises ultimate braking, as well as offering a rather vague feel when pushing hard on the track.

Ground clearance is, again, ample for the road, but is a limit on track. Not that this bothered John Reynolds – the British racer won the 1990 600cc Supercup

championship on a lightning-quick Team Green ZZ-R600.

Throughout the 1990s, the ZZ-R was a consistently strong seller, even when Kawasaki's own ZX-6R pushed the ZZ-R back into a sports-touring role. The ZZ-R's excellent road manners, high equipment levels and sound build-quality made it the ideal choice for many high-mileage riders.

Minor modifications over the years have further refined the ZZ-R600 with a fuel gauge, clock, suspension damping adjustment and improved power delivery.

Top speed:	249km/h (155mph)
Engine type:	599cc, l/c inline-four, 16-valve, DOHC
Maximum power:	73kW (98bhp) at 12,000rpm
Frame type:	twin-spar aluminium
Tyre sizes:	front 120/60 17, rear 160/60 17
Final drive:	chain
Gearbox:	six-speed
Weight:	195kg (430lb)

Kawasaki ZX-636R Ninja

For 2002, Kawasaki took a novel approach to the highly competitive 600cc sports class – it simply bored-out its ZX-6R engine by 2mm (0.07in) to 68mm (2.7in), making the capacity 37cc bigger. This was made possible by an earlier change – the 2000-model update had replaced the old engine's steel liners with a plated aluminium bore. The new design gave extra space round the cylinders, which allowed the larger bore. The engine cases had to be modified to provide more gasket area around the larger cylinders, and the cylinder head was modified to provide the optimum combustion chamber shape for the new bore size. The rest of the ZX-636R is largely unchanged from the 2001-model ZX-6R.

Top speed:	257km/h (160mph)
Engine type:	636cc, l/c inline-four, 16-valve, DOHC
Maximum power:	N\A
Frame type:	twin-spar aluminium
Tyre sizes:	front 120/65 17, rear 180/55 17
Final drive:	chain
Gearbox:	six-speed
Weight:	171kg (377lb)

Kawasaki W650

While it looks anything but, the W650 is one of Kawasaki's most recent designs. Launched in 1999 it uses the retro styling of Kawasaki's W1, first built in the 1960s. Its air-cooled parallel twin engine has rounded cases and fins designed to re-create 30-year-old styling, and uses a bevel drive shaft to operate the overhead cam. The rest of the bike also harks back to the past. The fuel tank wears rubber kneepads, the low-slung silencers use a classic peashooter design, and the rubber fork gaitors and kickstart would almost convince the casual observer that this was indeed a bike from the 1960s. The W650 isn't totally devoid of modern components though. The engine has electric start, and the front disc brake is decidedly up-to-date.

Top speed:	177km/h (110mph)
Engine type:	675cc, a/c parallel twin, eight-valve, SOHC
Maximum power:	37kW (50bhp) at 7000rpm
Frame type:	steel-tube double cradle
Tyre sizes:	front 100/90 19, rear 130/80 18
Final drive:	chain
Gearbox:	five-speed
Weight:	195kg (430lb)

Kawasaki ZR-7

The ZR-7 was first introduced in 1999, although the engine specification could have been from 25 years earlier. That's because the ZR-7 is based around a slightly updated version of the Z750 engine of 1973.

The air-cooled four-cylinder engine is decidedly low-tech, but it offers economical, reliable running, with a lazy, flexible power delivery.

The chassis is more up-to-date, but not by much. A steel-tube cradle frame is more than stiff enough for the power, and a monoshock rear suspension unit is adjustable for preload. The twin-piston front brake calipers aren't peformance parts, but provide sufficient stopping power, and the modern tyre sizes allow decent sport-touring rubber to be fitted.

Grippy rubber just shows up the lacklustre nature of the rest of the chassis though, and the ZR-7 quickly runs out of ground clearance in fast bends.

However, the ZR-7 does win out in the equipment stakes. The fuel tank holds a massive 22 litres (4.8 gal), the exhaust is long-lasting stainless steel and in addition there's a large storage space under the comfortable dual seat.

For 2001, Kawasaki launched a faired version of the ZR-7, the ZR-7S. While the small half-fairing certainly improved the bike's practicality and distance capability, the

extra weight didn't help either the engine or the brakes, and the ZR-7S was still outclassed by Suzuki's Bandit, Yamaha's Fazer and the faired Honda Hornet 'S' in almost every way.

Kept in a low-performance commuting or novice bike role, the ZR-7 is just about up to the job. But it is the superiority of its competitors that relegates the ZR-7 to the bottom of many riders' list. Having said that, the ZR-7 has proved popular in some continental markets: extreme customized ZR-7s are, strangely, a common sight in France.

Top speed:	201km/h (125mph)
Engine type:	738cc, a/c inline-four, eight-valve, DOHC
Maximum power:	56kW (75bhp) at 9500rpm
Frame type:	steel-tube double cradle
Tyre sizes:	front 120/70 17, rear 160/60 17
Final drive:	chain
Gearbox:	five-speed
Weight:	202kg (444lb)

Kawasaki ZX-7R Ninja

The styling of the ZX-7R is pure sportsbike. With its twin headlight race fairing, yawning ram-air intakes and hunched, aggressive poise, it looks every inch the racer. And with a high-revving, 748cc four-cylinder engine tucked inside a massively strong aluminium twin-spar frame, the spec sheet seems to back up these impressions. A fat 190-section rear tyre, fully adjustable upside-down front forks and six-piston Tokico brake calipers are nothing more than you'd expect.

But the ZX-7R is less thrilling to ride. Unchanged since its launch in 1996, the ZX-7R has fallen behind in the horsepower and weight stakes, so its 91kW (122bhp) peak power output has to propel 203kg (448lb)of sportsbike.

This relatively poor power-to-weight ratio makes the ZX-7R feel slower than its competitors, such as Suzuki's GSX-R750. Even a modern 600 like Kawasaki's own ZX-6R is lighter, faster and more lively, although the ZX-7R's larger engine produces more low-down torque.

But the ZX-7R's chassis makes up for some of its dynamic drawbacks. The front end is very stable, helped by a forward weight bias, high-quality suspension and strong brakes. The fully adjustable rear suspension works well too, and the stiff aluminium frame, together with the compact mass of the bike, makes it fell planted in fast corners. The six-piston brake calipers are disappointing though, and don't have the power of many competing designs.

Despite its slightly lacklustre road performance, the ZX-7R has performed better than expected in Superbike racing. Japanese rider Akira Yanagawa was a common sight in the late 1990s, dicing at the front of World Superbike races on the distinctive green Kawasaki.

Kawasaki's WSB race bikes were based around a race version of the ZX-7R, the ZX-7RR, equipped with flat-slide carburettors and a close-ratio gearbox. This limited edition bike was, like Honda's RC45, a homologation model – it was sold to the public purely to make the bike eligible for WSB entries.

Top speed:	266km/h (165mph)
Engine type:	748cc, l/c inline-four, 16-valve, DOHC
Maximum power:	91kW (122bhp) at 11,400rpm
Frame type:	twin-spar aluminium
Tyre sizes:	front 120/70 17, rear 190/50 17
Final drive:	chain
Gearbox:	six-speed
Weight:	203kg (448lb)

Kawasaki Drifter 800

In a market dominated by retro designs, the Drifter range is notable for its extreme styling. Designed to look like nothing less than the 1940s Indian Chief motorcycles, the Drifter 800 looks like nothing else currently available, except the 1500 version. For such a dated-looking machine, the design is completely modern. The engine is a liquid-cooled V-twin, with four valves per cylinder and a single overhead cam valve-train. The steel-tube chassis is styled like a 1940s hardtail, with no rear suspension, but there's a hidden monoshock spring/damper unit controlling the movement of the braced swingarm. The forward foot controls, wide bars and comfy seat are ideal for slow-speed cruising.

Top speed:	177km/h (110mph)
Engine type:	805cc, l/c V-twin, eight-valve, SOHC
Maximum power:	42kW (56bhp) at 7500rpm
Frame type:	steel-tube double cradle
Tyre sizes:	front 130/90 16, rear 140/90 16
Final drive:	chain
Gearbox:	five-speed
Weight:	246kg (542lb)

Kawasaki VN800

The VN800 Classic is a stylish custom cruiser, designed to look like a Harley-Davidson. Powered by a modern, liquid-cooled V-twin engine with four valves per cylinder, the VN engine is a development of the reliable, long-running VN750 engine. In this application, it allows the long wheelbase, low-slung cruiser to top 169km/h (105mph), while providing smooth low- to mid-range power. The Classic differs from the base VN800 mostly in the styling, although it has the 40cm (16in) spoked wheels of the Drifter rather than the 53cm (21in) front wheel of the VN. Deep, valanced mudguards, a chromed air-filter housing and fat fork shrouds complete the Classic's authentic styling. It is an unremarkable bike to ride, best used for round-town cruising.

Top speed:	177km/h (110mph)
Engine type:	805cc, l/c V-twin, eight-valve, SOHC
Maximum power:	42kW (56bhp) at 7500rpm
Frame type:	steel-tube double cradle
Tyre sizes:	front 130/90 16, rear 140/90 16
Final drive:	chain
Gearbox:	five-speed
Weight:	235kg (518lb)

Kawasaki ZX-9R

Once the king of the open-class sportsbike, Kawasaki had not done well in the class since the GPZ900R was overtaken by Yamaha's FZR1000 EXUP in the late 1980s. Bikes like the ZX-10 and ZZ-R1100 were immensely fast, but didn't have the handling to match bikes like the FZR1000 or Honda's later FireBlade.

So much was expected from the first ZX-9R, the B1 model, which appeared in 1994. Broadly based upon the ZXR750, the ZX-9R was, again, extremely fast and powerful, but its aluminium beam frame, upside-down front forks and front ram-air intake meant it looked much more like a sportsbike. Unfortunately, at 215kg (474lb), it was too heavy for sports riding, and didn't trouble Honda's CBR900RR FireBlade too much.

By 1998 though, Kawasaki had thoroughly overhauled the ZX-9R, increasing power again and cutting weight to an impressive 183kg. Unfortunately, Yamaha's R1 had just been launched, moving the class up another step in terms of power and handling.

By 2001, the ZX-9R had been through another makeover, and although it still wasn't at the cutting edge of unlimited-class sports machines, it remained a fast, refined road bike. The extra mass over bikes like the R1 and FireBlade kept the ZX-9R more stable, while the additional space and larger fairing made it a useful, fast sports touring machine. The 113kW (152bhp) engine used a conventional 16-valve inline-four layout pulling strongly through the rev range.

The chassis was composed and stable, with plushly damped suspension, although the steering was rather ponderous and the six-piston brakes weren't the best in the class.

For 2002, the ZX-9R underwent another minor update. New improved four-piston Nissin brakes replaced the six-piston Tokicos, while a stronger frame and braced swingarm further enhanced handling. New ZX-12R styled headlights and air intake sharpened the ZX-9R's styling, but the whole package was still some way behind the FireBlade, R1 and Suzuki's GSX-R1000.

Top speed:	274km/h (170mph)
Engine type:	899cc, l/c inline-four, 16-valve, DOHC
Maximum power:	113kW (152bhp) at 11,000rpm
Frame type:	twin-spar aluminium
Tyre sizes:	front 120/70 17, rear 190/50 17
Final drive:	chain
Gearbox:	six-speed
Weight:	186kg (410lb

Kawasaki GTR1000

Kawasaki's large-capacity touring bike, the GTR1000 is a rather dated design, first introduced in 1986. The GTR's engine is a development of the GPZ1000RX sportsbike motor, itself derived from the GPZ900R. Producing almost 73kW (98bhp), this strong motor provides excellent performance, although the delivery is rather revvy. A six-speed gearbox drives through a maintenance-free shaft drive, and the engine breathes through 32mm (1.3in) carburettors and a four-into-two exhaust system. The chassis is a typical touring design. The conventional suspension is soft for comfort, and does allow a degree of wallow in fast corners, while the twin piston front brake calipers struggle to halt such a heavy machine.

Top speed:	233km/h (145mph)
Engine type:	997cc, l/c inline-four, 16-valve, DOHC
Maximum power:	73kW (98bhp) at 9000rpm
Frame type:	steel-tube spine
Tyre sizes:	front 110/80 18, rear 150/80 16
Final drive:	shaft
Gearbox:	six-speed
Weight:	270kg (595lb)

Kawasaki GPZ1100

Not to be confused with the air-cooled GPZ1100 of the early 1980s, this modern sports-touring bike was first released in 1995. Powered by a detuned version of the mighty ZZ-R1100 engine, the GPZ1100 offered a cheaper, more touring-biased mix than the ZZ-R1100, with almost as much performance. A protective full fairing, upright riding position and comfy dual seat are ideal for two-up fast touring duties, and the well-designed chassis is capable of impressively sporty riding. Twin front disc brakes offer strong, predictable braking, and the GPZ is the only Kawasaki with an optional factory-fit anti-lock braking system. The ABS GPZ1100 weighs 10kg (22lb) more, but offers more confident stopping on uncertain road surfaces.

Top speed:	224km/h (140mph)
Engine type:	1052cc, l/c inline-four, 16-valve, DOHC
Maximum power:	92kW (123bhp) at 9500rpm
Frame type:	steel-tube spine
Tyre sizes:	front 120/70 17, rear 170/60 17
Final drive:	chain
Gearbox:	six-speed
Weight:	242kg (534lb)

Kawasaki ZZR1100

For the best part of the 1990s, Kawasaki's ZZ-R1100 was the fastest, most powerful production motorcycle available. Launched to an unsuspecting public in 1990, the ZZ-R11 staggered everyone who rode it with its amazing acceleration and startling 275km/h (171mph) top speed. Kawasaki organized the press riding launch in the US state of Arizona, and there are legendary tales of over-zealous journalists being thrown in jail after being clocked well over 240km/h (150mph) by US traffic police on the state highways.

Kawasaki Heavy Industries produces a wide range of aeronautical products, from aircraft and fast trains to space rockets, so its aerodynamic design experience is extensive. And it's the aerodynamic design of the ZZ-R1100 which makes it so fast – although the 110kW (147bhp) engine certainly helps. The rounded, bulbous bodywork cuts smoothly through the air, the full fairing also protecting the rider in a bubble of relatively still air.

There is nothing exceptional about the engine design – the inline-four, 16-valve liquid-cooled design is developed from the ZX-10, which derived from the GPZ1000RX and GPZ900R of the mid-1980s. But the way the motor produces power all the way though the mid-range is incredibly impressive, and the maximum power of 110kW (147bhp) is still respectable more than a decade after it was introduced.

The chassis is up to handling the engine's power, but its sheer mass and bulk

prevents excessively sporty riding. The brakes work well, but can feel overwhelmed by the physics of stopping more than 300kg (66lb) of bike and rider from 275km/h (171mph). Softly sprung, plush front forks are adjustable for spring preload and rebound damping, as is the rear monoshock, but it is difficult to adjust out the vague, slightly wallowy feel of the hefty Kawasaki accelerating hard out of bends.

Two-up fast motorway work is the ZZ-R11's forte. The low, spacious dual seat has plenty of room for two, and the aerodynamic screen and fairing guide wind and weather over both rider and pillion.

Top speed:	275km/h (171mph)
Engine type:	1052cc, l/c inline-four, 16-valve, DOHC
Maximum power:	110kW (147bhp) at 10,500rpm
Frame type:	twin-spar aluminium
Tyre sizes:	front 120/70 17, rear 180/55 17
Final drive:	chain
Gearbox:	six-speed
Weight:	233kg (514lb)

Kawasaki ZRX1100

L aunched in 1997, the ZRX1100 is a handsome retro-styled musclebike powered by a de-tuned ZZ-R1100 engine. Producing almost 75kW (100bhp), the heavyweight engine lost the ram-air intake system of the ZZ-R1100, and has redesigned top-end components to move power and torque lower down the rev range. It is installed in a basic steel-tube cradle frame, which is stiff enough to offer good handling, but is also heavy. Good-quality suspension units, including piggyback rear shocks and 43mm (1.7in) forks give a rather soft ride, and the tubular aluminium rear swingarm is both stylish and effective. Tokico six-piston front brake calipers don't really offer much more performance than competing four-piston designs.

Top speed:	224km/h (140mph)
Engine type:	1052cc, l/c inline-four, 16-valve, DOHC
Maximum power:	73kW (98bhp) at 8500rpm
Frame type:	steel-tube double cradle
Tyre sizes:	front 120/70 17, rear 170/60 17
Final drive:	chain
Gearbox:	five-speed
Weight:	222kg (488lb)

Kawasaki ZRX1200R

Introduced in 2001 as a replacement for the ZRX1100, the ZRX1200R is much more of an update than it looks. Externally similar to the 1100, the ZRX1200R had a host of engine changes, all aimed at modernizing the design and improving power delivery. The 112cc capacity increase to 1,164cc was made possible by replacing the old engine's steel cylinder liners with a plated aluminium block, but the altered block meant new crankcases. The chassis was less radically altered. A stiffer swingarm and revised shock positioning, with slightly longer wheelbase, improved stability. The neat headlight fairing was retained on this ZRX1200R model, and instruments and controls were similar. Kawasaki also produced an unfaired ZRX1200.

Top speed:	233km/h (145mph)
Engine type:	1164cc, l/c inline-four, 16-valve, DOHC
Maximum power:	89kW (120bhp) at 8500rpm
Frame type:	steel-tube double cradle
Tyre sizes:	front 120/70 17, rear 180/55 17
Final drive:	chain
Gearbox:	five-speed
Weight:	223kg (490lb)

Kawasaki ZRX 1200S

Kawasaki extended its retro musclebike lineup with this 'muscle tourer'. Essentially the ZRX1200R with a larger half-fairing, the 1200S was a straightforward way to produce a new all-rounder. The curvaceous half-fairing offers effective wind protection, guiding the blast up and over the rider. A twin-beam reflector headlight gives excellent illumination, and wide-set mirrors further improve usability. A revised dashboard includes a temperature and fuel gauge. These changes make the ZRX1200S a good choice for middle-distance touring, although the 140 mile range of the 19 litre tank isn't particularly impressive. The 1200S carries some extra weight over the ZRX1200R, but handles and performs almost identically.

Top speed:	241km/h (150mph)
Engine type:	1164cc, l/c inline-four, 16-valve, DOHC
Maximum power:	89kW (120bhp) at 8500rpm
Frame type:	steel-tube double cradle
Tyre sizes:	front 120/70 17, rear 180/55 17
Final drive:	chain
Gearbox:	five-speed
Weight:	227kg (499lb)

Kawasaki ZZR1200

The introduction of Kawasaki's ZX-12R in 2000 had overshadowed the ZZ-R1100, reclassifying it as a sports-touring machine. Kawasaki decided to revamp the ZZ-R1100 into a more obviously touring-biased machine for 2002. The increased-capacity engine is similar to the ZRX1200 engine, itself a variant on the ZZ-R1100 motor. The larger bore and stroke means the crankcases and cylinders are modifed, and most of the ZZ-R1200 engine has been modified from the older 1100. The frame and back end of the 1200 look similar to the older bike, but the front fairing is a more protective touring item with a taller, wider screen. Taller bars give a more upright riding position, and the foot pegs are lower than the ZZ-R1100 for improved comfort.

Top speed:	257km/h (160mph)
Engine type:	1164cc, l/c inline-four, 16-valve, DOHC
Maximum power:	86kW (115bhp) at 8000rpm
Frame type:	twin-spar aluminium
Tyre sizes:	front 120/70 17, rear 180/55 17
Final drive:	chain
Gearbox:	six-speed
Weight:	256kg (564lb)

Kawasaki ZX-12R

Kawasaki had long owned the 'fastest motorcycle' crown with its ZZ-R1100, until Honda's Blackbird then Suzuki's Hayabusa moved the class on. The ZX-12R Ninja was Kawasaki's response. An all-new design, it uses a unique monocoque frame, together with a 142kW (190bhp) engine, the most powerful currently available. The chassis is aimed at speed: the frame is narrower than a twin-spar design, and houses the airbox and battery, saving space elsewhere. Aerodynamic bodywork is dominated by a massive ram-air scoop, and huge mirrors, small canard wings on the lower fairing and cast spoilers on the forks help the ZX-12R to a top speed of 299km/h (186mph). It is also more sporty than the Hayabusa or Blackbird.

Top speed:	299km/h (186mph)
Engine type:	1199cc, l/c inline-four, 16-valve, DOHC
Maximum power:	142kW (190bhp) at 10,500rpm
Frame type:	monocoque aluminium
Tyre sizes:	front 120/70 17, rear 200/50 17
Final drive:	chain
Gearbox:	six-speed
Weight:	210kg (463lb)

Kawasaki
VN1500 Classic

Kawasaki's take on the massive cruiser concept has a long history – the first VN1500 appeared in 1988, and has remained basically the same since. The massive V-twin engine at the heart of the VN is a rather high-tech design. Liquid-cooled, it has four valves per cylinder, and a single overhead camshaft per cylinder, while the latest model, since 2001, has been equipped with fuel-injection. But for all its technology, the engine feels rather asthmatic, producing only 48kW (65bhp), although it is very torquey at low revs. The chassis is a typical cruiser design – a low seat and pull-back handlebars give a cruising riding position. The chrome air-filter housing, dual exhausts and valanced mudguards make the VN look like an authentic US cruiser.

Top speed:	185km/h (115mph)
Engine type:	1470cc, l/c V-twin, eight-valve, SOHC
Maximum power:	48kW (65bhp) at 4700rpm
Frame type:	steel-tube cradle
Tyre sizes:	front 130/90 16, rear 150/80 16
Final drive:	shaft
Gearbox:	five-speed
Weight:	292kg (644lb)

Kawasaki Drifter 1500

Launched in 1999, at the same time as the Drifter 800, the Drifter 1500 looks very similar to its smaller sibling. Underneath the retro styling however, it is a very different machine.

Using the liquid-cooled eight-valve engine from the VN1500, the Drifter has a slow-revving, grunty power delivery, helped by its electronic fuel-injection system. A maintenance-free shaft drive transfers power to the wide 40cm (16in) back tyre and a five-speed gearbox is changed by a heel and toe shifter pedal.

The chassis is similar to the VN1500, with a hidden rear suspension system.

But it is the Drifter's styling which is most important. Taking its cues from the American Indian marque of the 1940s, the Kawasaki design team committed fully to the concept. At the front of the bike, a massive, deeply valanced mudguard shrouds almost the entire wire spoked front wheel, topped off by a small headlight and fat fork shrouds. A seamless teardrop fuel tank leads back to the well-padded solo seat, and another bizarrely deep mudguard.

The whole arrangement is underlined by a snaking, chromed exhaust pipe which ends in a fishtail slashcut pipe. The Drifter has less chrome plate than other cruisers – 1940s Indians didn't have much chrome either, and many metal parts are finished with a gloss black paint.

Riding the Drifter is much like riding many other large cruiser. The engine quickly revs out, and changing up at 3500rpm gives the best progress. Top speed is around 185km/h (115mph), but the wide bars and no wind protection makes keeping this speed up hard. There's little ground clearance, and the suspension and brakes are rather unsophisticated.

Kept in town or on slow highway cruises, however, the Drifter is a civilized ride. Many riders customize their Drifter with some of the extensive catalogue of factory and aftermarket custom parts available.

Top speed:	185km/h (115mph)
Engine type:	1470cc, l/c V-twin, eight-valve, SOHC
Maximum power:	48kW (65bhp) at 4700rpm
Frame type:	steel-tube cradle
Tyre sizes:	front 130/90 16, rear 150/80 16
Final drive:	shaft
Gearbox:	five-speed
Weight:	304kg (670lb)

KTM Sting

The Sting is a 125cc supermotard styled machine. Eligible for European learners to ride in restricted form, it can be de-restricted to produce more power than the standard 10kW (14bhp). A liquid-cooled single-cylinder two-stroke design, it uses reed valve induction and has a large expansion chamber exhaust to improve power delivery. The styling is borrowed from the firm's successful Duke supermotard, including the large, aggressive twin headlight nosecone. Massively stiff upside-down forks look like they're straight off a full works race machine, and a huge 320mm (12.6in) front brake disc with four-piston caliper gives superb stopping power. The Sting is fitted with 43cm (17in) spoked wheels with sticky sportsbike rubber.

Top speed:	121km/h (75mph)
Engine type:	125cc single-cylinder two-stroke
Maximum power:	10kW (14bhp) at 7500rpm
Frame type:	steel-tube double cradle
Tyre sizes:	front 110/70 17, rear 130/70 17
Final drive:	chain
Gearbox:	six-speed
Weight:	124kg (274lb)

KTM 300 EXC

KTM's EXC range is made up of dedicated competition enduro motorcycles. These machines are nominally road legal – many enduros have an on-road section, but they have only the very basic equipment required for road use, including a small headlight, speedo and tail-light. What the EXC is really designed for is difficult off-road conditions. The single-cylinder two-stroke engine is compact, light and powerful – ideal for off-road use. But the most important part of an off-road machine is the suspension, and the EXC is very well-equipped. WP upside-down forks and rear monoshock are very tough, high-spec parts, and together with dedicated off-road tyres, makes the 300EXC a superb off-road machine.

Top speed:	137km/h (85mph)
Engine type:	297cc, l/c single-cylinder two-stroke
Maximum power:	not available
Frame type:	chrome-moly steel-tube cradle
Tyre sizes:	front 90/90 21, rear 140/80 18
Final drive:	chain
Gearbox:	five-speed
Weight:	109kg (240lb)

KTM Duke

KTM's Duke was the machine that brought the Austrian firm to the attention of many riders in the late 1990s. Formerly restricted to niche off-road bikes, it was this supermotard-styled bike which gained KTM recognition as a major bike manufacturer.

The original Duke, launched in 1994 used a 610cc single-cylinder four-stroke engine in an off-road chassis, equipped with a distinctive twin headlight nosecone and 43cm (17in) wire spoked wheels. Its 41kW (55bhp) power and 145kg (320lb) mass made it an exciting ride, but it was only imported into the UK in limited numbers.

The latest Duke, the 640, was launched in 1999. It has an uprated 624cc version of the old four-valve engine, which produces similar power, but with more torque, in a similar steel-tube cradle chassis. WP upside-down forks and WP monoshock provide excellent handling, while stylish BBS 43cm (17in) cast wheels wear grippy sportsbike tyres. A massive 320mm (12.6in) front brake disc is matched to a single four-piston Brembo racing caliper, giving amazing braking power, helped by the tiny 145kg (320lb) mass. The outrageous nosecone is also still there, with a twin headlight design, and sweeping fuel tank.

On the road, the Duke excels in tight, twisty city streets or mountain passes, where its quick steering, long travel suspension and amazing brakes all work superbly.

Narrow uphill hairpin bends which can tie a 'proper' race-replica sportsbike in knots are easily dealt with on the Duke.

It is not really suited to longer trips though – there's little in the way of comfort or equipment, and the tiny fuel tank only holds 11.5 litres (2.5 gal) – barely enough for 160km (100 miles) between refills.

The Duke's high-specification chassis parts also have a price penalty – it is an expensive machine, costing as much as some 600cc four-cylinder sportsbikes.

Top speed:	170km/h (105mph)
Engine type:	624cc, l/c single-cylinder, four-valve, SOHC
Maximum power:	41kW (55bhp) at 7250rpm
Frame type:	chrome-moly steel-tube double cradle
Tyre sizes:	front 120/70 17, rear 160/60 17
Final drive:	chain
Gearbox:	five-speed
Weight:	145kg (320lb)

KTM LC4

KTM's LC4 range includes three variations – a Supermoto-styled machine, an enduro spec competition bike and a Paris-Dakar replica desert racer. All three used the same single-cylinder four-stroke 609cc engine, but the latest versions use the uprated 625cc engine, confusingly called the 640 range. The Enduro follows a similar route to the firm's EXC range, with wire-spoked wheels wearing off-road tyres and a small Brembo front brake disc. The strong power delivery of the single-cylinder engine and the high-quality suspension and brakes is a devastating package in the hands of an experienced rider. A small fuel tank and constant vibration from the single-cylinder engine means the LC4 is rather impractical on the road.

Top speed:	169km/h (105mph)
Engine type:	625cc, l/c single-cylinder, four-valve, SOHC
Maximum power:	36kW (48bhp) at 7500rpm
Frame type:	chrome-moly steel-tube double cradle
Tyre sizes:	front 90/90 21, rear 140/80 18 [Adventure]
Final drive:	chain
Gearbox:	five-speed
Weight:	154kg (340lb) [Adventure], 137kg (302lb) [Supermoto]

Laverda 750S

The Laverda 750S was the last version of the bike which relaunched Laverda in 1991, the 650 Sport. A heavily revised parallel twin engine in an up-to-date chassis, the 750S captured many riders' hearts with its high-class specification. The chassis was built around a twin-beam aluminium frame. Paioli upside-down front forks, a Paioli monoshock, Marchesini wheels and Brembo brakes are as fine as anything fitted to Ducati or Bimota machines. The result is an exquisitely well-balanced machine, with excellent handling. Unfortunately, the Laverda is let down by its engine. Based on an extremely old design, it has a revvy, harsh delivery, despite its fuel-injection.

Top speed:	240km/h (149mph)
Engine type:	748cc, l/c parallel twin, eight-valve, DOHC
Maximum power:	69kW (92bhp) at 9000rpm
Frame type:	aluminium twin-spar
Tyre sizes:	front 120/60 17, rear 160/60 17
Final drive:	chain
Gearbox:	six-speed
Weight:	192kg (423lb)

Laverda 750S Formula

Laverda's Formula 750S is essentially a factory-built special edition of the basic Formula, with extensive engine tuning and even more special chassis componentry.

The original Formula was a 650, built in 1996, with the 750 Formula following a year later in 1997.

The engine work was more extensive than most factory specials, and took the Formula almost to a race tune straight from the showroom. Uprated cams, revised fuel-injection settings and carbon-fibre Termignoni silencers all boost top-end power to an impressive claimed figure of 69kW (92bhp) – almost as much as the more successful Ducati 748, another 750-class twin.

The chassis also compares well with the 748, being considerably lighter, and with suspension and braking components every bit as impressive as the Ducati.

Fully adjustable Paioli upside-down forks and monoshock, fully-floating Brembo racing brakes and lightweight Marchesini wheels all play their part in giving the Formula impeccable track manners and sharp handling.

The polished aluminium beam frame looks much more impressive than the Ducati's thin steel-tube affair, although the Ducati frame is stiffer than it looks. A single-seat

race-style fairing incorporates stylish cooling louvres and twin endurance-style headlights, and is finished in Laverda orange, the firm's distinctive racing colour. Despite the impressive spec, and some success in endurance racing, the Formula still suffered from the weakness and revvy nature of the old parallel twin-engine design, and it was never as successful as Ducati's 748.

Indeed, at the time of writing, Laverda's future as a whole is very unclear - the troubled firm was bought by Aprilia in 2001, and there is, sadly, little sign of any new Laverda motorcycles being produced in the immediate future.

Top speed:	242km/h (150mph)
Engine type:	748cc, l/c parallel twin, eight-valve, DOHC
Maximum power:	69kW (92bhp) at 9000rpm
Frame type:	aluminium twin-spar
Tyre sizes:	front 120/60 17, rear 160/60 17
Final drive:	chain
Gearbox:	six-speed
Weight:	187kg (411lb)

Moto Guzzi Nevada

The Nevada is Moto Guzzi's smallest bike, offering an entry-level choice to the Italian marque. Despite its 744cc capacity, the Nevada has a rather lazy engine performance, producing just over 34kW (45bhp). The elderly air-cooled transverse V-twin design is largely similar to the original V-7 engine of 1967, although it was revised in 1977, modern materials and a fuel-injection system giving a small performance boost over older models. Overhead pushrod valves and the two large pistons keep engine revs low, and the Nevada is best ridden on the ample low-down torque, ideal for its cruising role. The Nevada chassis is built around a basic steel-tube frame, with kicked-out cruiser-style front forks and twin rear shocks.

Top speed:	177km/h (110mph)
Engine type:	744cc, a/c 90° transverse V-twin, four-valve, OHV
Maximum power:	34kW (46bhp) at 6200rpm
Frame type:	steel-tube double cradle
Tyre sizes:	front 100/90 18, rear 130/90 16
Final drive:	shaft
Gearbox:	five-speed
Weight:	182kg (401lb)

Moto Guzzi Quota

First released in 1992 as a 1000, then revamped in 1998 as an 1100, the Quota combines Guzzi's ubiquitous V-twin powerplant with dated bodywork and off-road type suspension. The rather agricultural engine is very tractable, although top-end power delivery is less than impressive. The riding position offers a degree of comfort for rider and passenger, and if equipped with aftermarket luggage, the Quota makes an acceptable touring option. The 20-litre (4.4 gal) fuel tank could be larger, but the Quota's typical 40–50mpg consumption still allows well over 240km (150 miles) to a tankful. Rival machines like BMW's R1150GS all offer improved performance and refinement, though, and make a better choice for most riders.

Top speed:	190km (118mph)
Engine type:	1064cc, a/c 90° transverse V-twin, four-valve, OHV
Maximum power:	53kW (71bhp) at 6400rpm
Frame type:	square steel-tube double cradle
Tyre sizes:	front 90/90 21, rear 130/80 17
Final drive:	shaft
Gearbox:	five-speed
Weight:	245kg (540lb)

Moto Guzzi V10 Centauro Sport

The Centauro is a curious looking motorcycle, with its sweeping fuel tank, broad seat and bulbous tail unit. Launched to celebrate Guzzi's 75th anniversary in 1997, the V10 is a mix of expensive chassis components, bizarre styling and traditional Guzzi engineering. The engine is perhaps the best feature, based on the Guzzi Daytona eight-valve sportsbike engine, replacing the usual Guzzi pushrod valves with an overhead cam design. With Weber fuel-injection, it produces 15kW (20bhp) more than the pushrod engine, with smoother power delivery. The chassis is composed of the best suspension and brake components from WP, Brembo and Bitubo, which all perform well while not disguising the Centauro's weight.

Top speed:	225km/h (140mph)
Engine type:	992cc, a/c 90° transverse V-twin, eight-valve, SOHC
Maximum power:	71kW (95bhp) at 7400rpm
Frame type:	steel-tube spine
Tyre sizes:	front 120/70 17, rear 160/60 17
Final drive:	shaft
Gearbox:	five-speed
Weight:	224kg (493lb)

Moto Guzzi California EV

The California EV is the latest interpretation of the long-running California series. Refined, with improved build quality and finish, it is essentially the same as the previous models. The air-cooled transverse V-twin engine has a torquey power delivery, but is weak at the top-end. The design's longitudinal crank allows a simple path to the final shaft drive, reducing power losses. There are two versions of the EV: the basic model, with chromed engine bars and cruiser-style cissy bar and pullback handlebars, and a touring version, which has a large windshield. Moto Guzzi released a special version of its California in 2001 to celebrate the firm's 80th anniversary. This California EV 80 is fitted with exclusive leather saddlebags, seat and bar grips.

Top speed:	193km/h (120mph)
Engine type:	1064cc, a/c 90° transverse V-twin, four-valve, OHV
Maximum power:	54kW (72bhp) at 6400rpm
Frame type:	steel-tube double cradle
Tyre sizes:	front 110/90 18, rear 150/70 17
Final drive:	shaft
Gearbox:	five-speed
Weight:	251kg (553lb)

Moto Guzzi California Jackal

The California Jackal is a cruiser-styled machine based around the California engine and chassis. The traditional Moto Guzzi air-cooled transverse V-twin engine is fitted to a basic steel-tube frame with simple suspension and brakes bolted on. The performance from the elderly engine is rather lazy, although what power there is, is produced well down the rev range, allowing relaxed progress. The engine breathes through a basic fuel-injection system, but the power delivery can be rather flat at low revs. The Jackal is a fairly handsome machine, its kicked-out front forks holding a wire spoked 46cm (18in) front wheel and a single front brake disc. Deep, curvaceous mudguards and a dash of chrome plate round off the bodywork.

Top speed:	193km/h (120mph)
Engine type:	1064cc, a/c 90° transverse V-twin, four-valve, OHV
Maximum power:	54kW (72bhp) at 6400rpm
Frame type:	steel-tube double cradle
Tyre sizes:	front 110/90 18, rear 140/80 17
Final drive:	shaft
Gearbox:	five-speed
Weight:	246kg (541lb)

Moto Guzzi California Special

The Moto Guzzi California Special is another variation on the California theme, launched in 1998. Moto Guzzi's transverse V-twin air-cooled engine is here fitted to a cruiser-styled chassis, with pullback handlebars, low-slung seat and chromed twin shock rear suspension. A five-speed shaft drive transmission delivers the 1064cc engine's power to the rear wire-spoked wheel. The California Special uses an integrated braking system. The twin front Brembo 320mm (12.6in) discs and four-piston calipers are linked to the rear twin-piston caliper by a delay control valve, allowing controlled, powerful stopping by using both hand and foot levers together. The California Special was replaced by the California Special Sport in 2001.

Top speed:	193km/h (120mph)
Engine type:	1064cc, a/c 90° transverse V-twin, four-valve, OHV
Maximum power:	54kW (72bhp) at 6400rpm
Frame type:	steel-tube double cradle
Tyre sizes:	front 110/90 18, rear 140/80 17
Final drive:	shaft
Gearbox:	five-speed
Weight:	251kg (553lb)

Moto Guzzi 1100 Sport Injection

Moto Guzzi's 1100 Sport Injection was an attempt to produce a sporting machine using the firm's dated OHV engine design. Launched in 1996 as a replacement for the carburettor-equipped 1100 Sport, it was a budget version of the powerful Daytona 1000 race replica. While the Daytona had an OHC four-valve design, the 1100 Sport stuck with the OHV design common to the rest of Guzzi's range. The chassis was equipped with high-quality WP suspension and lightweight wheels wore sporting radial tyres. The result, with the slow-revving, rather agricultural engine, was a sportsbike full of character which could be ridden surprisingly quickly on the road, where its extra weight ensured a stable ride through fast bends.

Top speed:	230km/h (143mph)
Engine type:	1064cc, a/c 90° transverse V-twin, four-valve, OHV
Maximum power:	67kW (90bhp) at 7800rpm
Frame type:	steel-tube backbone
Tyre sizes:	front 120/70 17, rear 160/70 17
Final drive:	shaft
Gearbox:	five-speed
Weight:	221kg (487lb)

Moto Guzzi V11 Sport

Moto Guzzi engineers did their best with limited resources to produce the V11, a naked retro sportster based around the firm's air-cooled V-twin powertrain. Quality chassis parts, including Brembo Oro brakes, Marzocchi upside-down forks and a WP rear shock help bring the basic chassis up to a respectable level of performance. Despite the engine and frame being based on a 30-year-old design, the V11 rides well. An updated six-speed gearbox and lightened clutch action are a big improvement over previous models, and the fuel-injection system is smooth and hiccup-free. An enclosed shaft delivers drive to the rear wheel. A limited-edition Mandello Rosso version has special paint and carbon-fibre performance parts.

Top speed:	219kW (136mph)
Engine type:	1064cc, a/c transverse 90° V-twin, four-valve, OHV
Maximum power:	68kW (91bhp) at 7800rpm
Frame type:	steel-tube box section
Tyre sizes:	front 120/70 17, rear 170/60 17
Final drive:	shaft
Gearbox:	six-speed
Weight:	219kg (481lb)

MV Agusta Brutale

This striking naked machine is built around the F4 sportsbike platform, with redesigned bodywork. The styling is radical and aggressive (hence the name), dominated by the hunched profile of the tank and the distinctive double parabola headlamp. The engine is the same radial-valved fuel-injected design as fitted to the F4, producing an impressive 95kW (127bhp). A stiff Tig-welded steel trellis frame mounts top of the range Showa upside-down forks and Sachs rear shock with a magnesium single-sided swingarm and Nissin six-piston brakes. But it's the styling of the Brutale, as well as the high-spec components that make it so typically Latin. The Oro was a limited edition version, and a lower-spec 'S' (Strada) version is also available.

Top speed:	249km/h (155mph)
Engine type:	749cc, l/c inline-four, 16-valve, DOHC
Maximum power:	95kW (127bhp) at 12,500rpm
Frame type:	chrome-moly steel-tube trellis
Tyre sizes:	front 120/65 17, rear 190/50 17
Final drive:	chain
Gearbox:	six-speed
Weight:	179kg (395lb)

MV Agusta F4S

From its unveiling in 1997, the MV Agusta F4S has caught bikers' imaginations like no machine since Ducati's 916. Both designs were penned by Massimo Tamburini. The styling and specification of the MV are unique. The deep red-and-silver gloss of the sleek bodywork cunningly combines smooth and angular shapes. The radical four-into-four exhaust terminates in a set of underseat silencers which give a glorious roar on the move. The F4's engine has the technical prowess to match its design. The cylinder head uses a distinctive radial valve design – the valve pairs are slightly splayed away from each other so the valve stems are at an angle. This allows a more efficient combustion chamber shape, but is difficult to manufacture.

Top speed:	283km/h (176mph)
Engine type:	749cc, l/c inline-four, 16-valve, DOHC
Maximum power:	102kW (137bhp) at 12,600rpm
Frame type:	chrome-moly steel-tube trellis
Tyre sizes:	front 120/65 17, rear 190/50 17
Final drive:	chain
Gearbox:	six-speed
Weight:	192kg (423lb)

MV Agusta F4 Senna

Claudio Castiglioni, the president of MV Agusta, was a close friend of Ayrton Senna, and has worked closely with the charitable Senna Foundation since the legendary F1 driver died in a crash at Imola in 1994. The F4 Senna is a limited edition of 300 machines, with all proceeds going to the Senna Foundation to help disadvantaged children. Based around the high-spec SPR version of the F4, it features the same engine and chassis, with a special black-and-red colour scheme and silver numbered plaque. The SPR engine has a higher rev ceiling, producing an impressive 109kW (146bhp). Stronger pistons and a lightened crankshaft allow the higher revs. Many chassis parts have been replaced with lighter, carbon-fibre parts.

Top speed:	293km/h (182mph)
Engine type:	749cc, l/c inline-four, 16-valve, DOHC
Maximum power:	109kW (146bhp) at 13,000rpm
Frame type:	chrome-moly steel-tube trellis
Tyre sizes:	front 120/65 17, rear 190/50 17
Final drive:	chain
Gearbox:	six-speed
Weight:	188kg (414lb)

MV Agusta F4SPR

The SPR version of the F4 is externally similar to the F4S. The upside-down front forks, single-sided swingarm and stunning bodywork are all identical to the basic bike, but many engine and chassis details have been modified to improve track performance. As on the Senna model, lighter, stronger Mahle forged pistons allow power to be produced at higher levels. The Weber-Marelli fuel-injection system of the F4 is adapted for higher revs, and a lighter crankshaft improves throttle response. Many chassis parts, including the front mudguard and the chain guards, are replaced by carbon-fibre parts, reducing weight by 4kg (8.8lb), and the innovative dash now includes a track chronometer function.

Top speed:	293km/h (182mph)
Engine type:	749cc, l/c inline-four, 16-valve, DOHC
Maximum power:	109kW (146bhp) at 13,000rpm
Frame type:	chrome-moly steel-tube trellis
Tyre sizes:	front 120/65 17, rear 190/50 17
Final drive:	chain
Gearbox:	six-speed
Weight:	188kg (414lb)

MZ Baghira

MZ first introduced this enduro-styled off-roader in 1997. The German firm's historical range of two-stroke engines were not suitable for a modern machine, so a Yamaha engine, the single-cylinder liquid-cooled motor from the XTZ660 Tenere, was used. The torquey, rugged design uses a five-valve cylinder head for efficient breathing and combustion, and the clever Yamaha Dual Intake System, which has one CV and one slide carb to give the best power delivery of both carb types. The Baghira chassis is basic, but effective. Long travel forks soak up off-road bumps, and a high-spec WP rear shock keeps the long box-section swingarm under control. Grimeca disc brakes are not particularly strong, but are designed for off-road use.

Top speed:	161km/h (100mph)
Engine type:	660cc, l/c single, five-valve, SOHC
Maximum power:	37kW (50bhp) at 6500rpm
Frame type:	steel-tube cradle
Tyre sizes:	front 90/90 21, rear 120/80 18
Final drive:	chain
Gearbox:	five-speed
Weight:	165kg (364lb)

MZ Mastiff

The Mastiff is basically the same bike as the Baghira off-road machine, with road wheels, tyres and brakes. The styling is more radical, with twin headlights enclosed in a tough wire cage, and a neat, short front mudguard. The 43cm (17in) wheels allow sticky sportsbike rubber to be fitted, and are better suited to road use. The Grimeca brakes are uprated too – the front brake has a larger 298mm (11.7in) floating disc, which gives much better stopping power. The suspension is the same spec as the Baghira – 45mm (1.7in) conventional front forks and a WP rear monoshock unit. As a budget introduction to the pleasures of supermotard riding, the Mastiff can be a good option. It is also available in a 24kW (33bhp) version for restricted license holders.

Top speed:	169km/h (105mph)
Engine type:	660cc, l/c single, five-valve, SOHC
Maximum power:	37kW (50bhp) at 6500rpm
Frame type:	steel-tube cradle
Tyre sizes:	front 120/60 17, rear 150/60 17
Final drive:	chain
Gearbox:	five-speed
Weight:	164kg (362lb)

Suzuki RGV250

The RGV250 ruled the 250cc two-stroke race-replica roost for most of the 1990s. First produced to replace the RG250 in 1989, the first RGV250, the K model, was an incredibly high-spec machine. A 90° V-twin two-stroke engine produced an amazing 48kW (65bhp), which was enough to make the featherweight RGV more exciting than most bikes two or even three times its capacity.

Perhaps the most interesting model is the 1991 M model. The Grands Prix styling was extended to every part of the bike, from the fully-adjustable upside-down front forks to the rear banana-style swingarm and twin-exit silencers on the right hand side. The full race fairing has swooping, aerodynamic lines, while the minimalist seat pad and low clip-on bars put the rider into an aggressive racing crouch.

The engine and chassis both bristle with state-of-the-art technology. A computerized power-valve system alters the engine's exhaust characteristics to suit different revs, while electronic solenoids in the flat-slide carbs further refine fuelling, giving optimum performance.

The four-piston front calipers and fully floating discs are almost too much for the RGV's 139kg (306lb) mass. Safe, powerful stopping is easily achieved with just one or two fingers of lever pressure. Wide, sticky radial tyres give the little Suzuki maximum grip on road or track.

It is on the track that the RGV250 is most rewarding. Extreme acceleration, braking and lean angles are practically compulsory, and the RGV has won more than its fair share of clubman race championships. The highly tuned engine is tricky to tune reliably, however; many race engines are unreliable and need expensive maintenance.

Later models, from 1997 onwards, use a revised, narrow angle 70º engine with ram-air intakes, electric start and a dry clutch. These were only sold in Japan, but appeared in several other markets via unofficial grey importers.

Top speed:	209km/h (130mph)
Engine type:	249cc, l/c 90° V-twin, two-stroke
Maximum power:	48kW (65bhp) at 10,500rpm
Frame type:	aluminium twin-spar
Tyre sizes:	front 110/70 17, rear 150/60 17
Final drive:	chain
Gearbox:	six-speed
Weight:	139kg (306lb)

Suzuki GS500E

A simple, basic commuter twin, the GS500E is the preferred choice of UK rider training schools, making it a familiar machine for many riders. Its low-tech DOHC air-cooled parallel twin engine is based on the GS450 twin engine of the late 1980s. Two-valve heads mean low-revving, torquey power delivery, but leave the GS500 rather asthmatic at higher revs. The frame is similarly unassuming – the steel frame is cheap to manufacture and tough, but adds weight. Basic suspension units offer capable if unsophisticated damping performance, but single disc brakes front and rear give dependable stopping power. Cheap to buy and run, most GS500s work hard as commuters, courier or training machines.

Top speed:	185km/h (115mph)
Engine type:	487cc, a/c parallel twin, four-valve, DOHC
Maximum power:	38kW (51bhp) at 9200rpm
Frame type:	square section steel-tube perimeter
Tyre sizes:	front 110/70 17, rear 130/70 17
Final drive:	chain
Gearbox:	six-speed
Weight:	173kg (381lb)

Suzuki GSF600 Bandit

The Bandit 600 virtually created the middleweight budget bike class when it appeared in 1995. Based around a similar design to the 1990 Bandit 400, the Bandit 600 used an oil-cooled engine in a basic steel frame. Budget suspension and braking components kept costs down, and the Bandit was a lively, capable performer. It had just enough power to count as a 'big' bike while remaining unthreatening for novices, so was a popular choice for post-test riders. The traditional round headlamp and chrome-finished exhaust were matched by a colour-coded frame and silver-finish engine which gave the Bandit a healthy dose of attitude. The first update for the Bandit, in 2000, had a new frame and updated TPS carburettors.

Top speed:	209km/h (130mph)
Engine type:	600cc, a/c inline-four, 16-valve, DOHC
Maximum power:	58kW (78bhp) at 10,500rpm
Frame type:	steel-tube double cradle
Tyre sizes:	front 120/60 17, rear 160/60 17
Final drive:	chain
Gearbox:	six-speed
Weight:	204kg (450lb)

Suzuki GSF600S Bandit

Introduced a year after the unfaired Bandit 600, the Bandit 'S' extended the practical use of the Bandit significantly by the simple expedient of fitting a frame-mounted half-fairing. Suddenly, what had been a bike best kept in town or on twisty back roads had an additional long-distance touring dimension.

Much of the 'S' was identical to the base bike. The engine is a variation of the GSX600F's powerplant, a 16-valve inline-four oil-cooled design which produces 58kW (78bhp) in this application. The long-running GSX engine is both reliable and economical, although the dated nature of the design shows in its performance compared to more modern liquid-cooled engines such as Yamaha's Fazer or Honda's Hornet 600.

This original 1996 Bandit 'S' had a rather anonymous square headlight fairing, and many riders preferred the styling of the naked bike. But the fairing improved comfort and weather protection at motorway crusing speeds, making the Bandit 'S' a useful budget tourer.

A model update in 2000 had a new, twin projector headlight fairing, and the new frame and engine modifications of the unfaired bike. The revamped fairing gave more modern styling, better wind protection and improved aerodynamics. Engine changes include new carburettors with TPS throttle position sensors, linked to a more advanced ignition system, and with a different exhaust design, giving the

engine an extra 3kW (4bhp) in the mid-range. But peak power remained the same at 58kW (78bhp), some way off the class standard of nearer 67kW (90bhp) in 2000.

Chassis modifications were similarly understated – a new frame design lowered the seat height, the brakes were slightly modified and the fuel capacity increased to 20 litres (4.4 gal).

The Bandit remained a popular choice after 2000, but stiff opposition from Honda's Hornet 'S' and Yamaha's Fazer badly affected sales.

Top speed:	217km/h (135mph)
Engine type:	600cc, a/c inline-four, 16-valve, DOHC
Maximum power:	58kW (78bhp) at 10,500rpm
Frame type:	steel-tube double cradle
Tyre sizes:	front 120/60 17, rear 160/60 17
Final drive:	chain
Gearbox:	six-speed
Weight:	208kg (459lb)

Suzuki GSX600F

The original GSX600F was launched in 1988 as a sportsbike. At that time, its specification was perfectly acceptable for a performance machine – all-enclosing bodywork, a 16-valve engine and monoshock rear suspension put it on a par with its peer group. Only the slightly bland styling marked the GSX out from its competitors.

By 1998, the GSX600F had been relegated to a more pedestrian budget sports tourer role. However, Suzuki gave it a wheels-up makeover anyway. The former 'jellymould' styling was radically altered, but was still not to every rider's taste. The engine and carburation received internal modifications to produce improved low and mid-range power production, at the cost of some top-end power. And a new stainless steel exhaust resists corrosion, while improving power.

The engine uses a combination of oil and air cooling. A high-capacity oil pump circulates engine oil through a large oil radiator to cool the engine internals, while fins on the cylinder block also remove heat. Suzuki claims this saves weight over a liquid-cooled engine, while remaining more efficient than an air-cooled design.

Compared with modern sports machines, the GSX will disappoint. The brakes are indifferent, while the low pegs reduce ground clearance and soon drag on the ground during committed cornering. The engine's lack of sophistication shows in its harsh, revvy power delivery, and it feels underpowered compared with more modern designs.

However, the GSX600F makes an acceptable budget tourer. A large 20-litre (4.4 gal) fuel tank gives an impressive fuel range of almost 320km (200 miles), while the broad dual seat offers spacious accommodation for rider and pillion.

The soft suspension gives a smooth ride and the relaxed steering geometry is very stable at the GSX600F's maximum speed of around 225km/h (140mph).

Twin-beam headlights provide excellent night-time illumination, and the full fairing protects the rider from high-speed wind blast.

Top speed:	225km/h (140mph)
Engine type:	600cc, a/c inline-four, 16-valve, DOHC
Maximum power:	60kW (80bhp) at 10,500rpm
Frame type:	steel spine
Tyre sizes:	front 120/70 17, rear 150/70 17
Final drive:	chain
Gearbox:	six-speed
Weight:	200kg (442lb)

Suzuki GSX-R600

Suzuki's first real attempt at a modern supersports 600-class machine, the GSX-R600 was an instant success when it first appeared in 1997. It looked virtually identical to the firm's long-running GSX-R750, and had the performance figures to match its radical race-replica styling.

The GSX-R600's engine and chassis were largely conventional – a 16-valve, liquid-cooled inline-four, mounted in an aluminium twin-spar chassis with a full race-style fairing. The 600 had conventional telescopic forks, the easiest way to tell it from its 750cc sibling.

This first GSX-R600 had very focused, sporting performance. The engine produced strong top-end power, but had to be revved constantly to make the best progress. And the sharp steering chassis was at its best on the track, its high pegs and cramped riding position ruling long-distance trips out for most riders.

By 2001, the GSX-R had fallen behind its competitors, especially Yamaha's R6, so an all-new model raised the middleweight Suzuki's game once more. The GSX-R600K had numerous updates over the previous model, although it was, again, visually identical to the GSX-R750, with the exception of the front forks. The 599cc engine is redesigned, with lightweight forged pistons and ceramic coated bores. A new SDTV fuel-injection system, like that on the GSX-R750 and 100 models, provides smooth, flawless power delivery.

SDTV stands for Suzuki Dual Throttle Valve, and refers to the two butterfly valves in each throttle body. One valve is connected to the throttle twistgrip while the other valve is controlled via an electric motor by the ECU module. This setup allows the ECU to optimize airflow into the engine for precise fuelling and power delivery. So if the rider slams his throttle control open, the secondary valve opens at a slower rate to maintain a higher airflow velocity, preventing stuttering and poor running.

The 2001 update once more put the lightweight GSX-R600 at the top of the 600cc sportsbike class, especially in terms of racetrack performance.

Top speed:	266km/h (165mph)
Engine type:	599cc, l/c inline-four, 16-valve, DOHC
Maximum power:	89kW (120bhp) at 13,000rpm
Frame type:	aluminium twin-spar
Tyre sizes:	front 120/70 17, rear 180/55 17
Final drive:	chain
Gearbox:	six-speed
Weight:	163kg (359lb)

Suzuki SV650S

When it first appeared in 1999, the SV650 was one of the highest-spec bikes in its class. An all-new purpose-designed V-twin engine housed in an aluminium trellis frame with sporty styling was much more advanced than competing bikes like the Bandit 600 and Kawasaki's ZR-7.

Suzuki extended the appeal of the SV by offering two versions. An unfaired SV650 is ideal for town use, but this half-faired version extends the SV's remit to include longer-distance commuting and light touring. Higher gearing gives an increased top speed, while lower handlebars and a twin headlamp fairing keeps wind stress off the rider, allowing relaxed high-speed cruising. The SV650S also has twin trip meters and an integrated cockpit dash.

The engine looks like a miniature version of the firm's TL1000 motor, the eight-valve, quad-cam design producing an impressive 52kW (70bhp), with a pleasing, torquey delivery. The chassis provides similarly easy handling, the conventional upside-down forks and rear monoshock providing soft, predictable damping while the light weight and sporty geometry mean the SV steers quickly. Twin front brake discs with two-piston Tokico calipers provide ample stopping power.

The naked version of the SV is 4kg (8.8lb) lighter than the faired 'S' model, and is also geared lower, giving a lower top speed and faster acceleration. The result is a markedly different bike: much livelier round town, and more fun to ride. The

engine and chassis is largely identical to the unfaired machine, although the different riding position gives a more sporting feel. The aluminium frame is more than stiff enough for the power output, and sporting radial tyres give sportsbike levels of grip.

As an all-round budget or novice machine, the SV650S is an excellent choice. But more sporting riders may find the V-twin motor short of outright power compared with four-cylinder rivals, although the narrow, firm chassis is as sporty as anything else in the budget middleweight class.

Top speed:	201km/h (125mph)
Engine type:	645cc, l/c 90° V-twin, eight-valve, DOHC
Maximum power:	52kW (70bhp) at 9000rpm
Frame type:	aluminium trellis
Tyre sizes:	front 120/60 17, rear 160/60 17
Final drive:	chain
Gearbox:	six-speed
Weight:	169kg (373lb)

Suzuki Burgman 650

Launched in 2002, Suzuki's Burgman 650 was an attempt to build on the success of the firm's smaller Burgman 400 and 250 scooters. Like its competitors, Honda's Silver Wing and Yamaha's T-Max, it uses a custom-designed parallel twin engine. This high-output design uses liquid-cooling, four-valve heads and fuel-injection to produce strong, clean power delivery. The Burgman uses a computer-controlled automatic gearbox, with selectable performance modes. The standard mode changes gear ratios at lower revs, for good economy, while a sports mode changes the ratios at higher revs for stronger acceleration. The variable belt transmission also has a 'manual' setting, allowing electronic selection of set ratios.

Top speed:	185km/h (115mph)
Engine type:	638cc, l/c parallel-twin, eight-valve, DOHC
Maximum power:	97kW (130bhp) at 9500rpm
Frame type:	steel-tube perimeter
Tyre sizes:	front 120/70 15, rear 160/60 14
Final drive:	belt
Gearbox:	computer-controlled variable automatic
Weight:	215kg (474lb)

Suzuki GSX750

The GSX750W is a handsome, retro-designed roadster based around the elderly oil-cooled inline-four engine design used in the GSX750 sports tourer. A steel-tube cradle frame, aluminium twin-shock swingarm and conventional forks provide capable if basic handling, and twin front brake discs allow strong stopping power. The 750cc engine capacity provides ample power and torque, and is a much more satisfying ride than smaller machines like Suzuki's Bandit 600. The well-proven oil-cooled engine is extremely reliable and economical, and the stylish design and impressive build quality make the GSX750 a suitable commuting and cruising alternative to machines like Kawasaki's ZR-7 or Honda's CB Seven-Fifty.

Top speed:	218km/h (135mph)
Engine type:	750cc, o/c inline-four, 16-valve, DOHC
Maximum power:	64kW (86bhp) at 9500rpm
Frame type:	steel-tube spine
Tyre sizes:	front 120/70 17, rear 170/60 17
Final drive:	chain
Gearbox:	six-speed
Weight:	201kg (443lb)

Suzuki
GSX-R750

Suzuki's GSX-R750 is one of the longest running superbikes available today, and it has gained a legendary reputation over the years. From the first GSX-R750, introduced in 1985, to the current 2002 model, there have been seven major updates, and many more minor changes.

In the process, power has gone up from an optimistic 75kW (100bhp) in 1985 to 105kW (141bhp) in 2000 and weight went up from 176kg (388lb) to 208kg (458lb) in 1992 before coming back down to 166kg (366lb) in 2000. The model shown here is the earlier sixth-generation model, with fuel-injection and 104kW (135bhp).

The latest model, along with the GSX-R600 and GSX-R1000, forms the most complete family of track-biased sporting machines available. Its on-paper statistics are startling – it weighs just 166kg (366lb), yet produces over 105kW (140bhp). The sharp, race-replica bodywork is wrapped around a taut, stiff aluminium twin-spar frame, with fully adjustable race suspension at either end.

The engine is a rather conventional design, with liquid-cooling, a 16-valve cylinder head and a six-speed gearbox. The fuel-injection is noteworthy though – its advanced dual throttle valve SDTV fuel-injection system uses a cunning combination of computer-controlled valves to match air flow to the engine's demands and the rider's throttle input, optimizing power production and delivery, while improving emissions control.

On the road, the GSX-R750 can be rather tiring, its focused nature and revvy power delivery making it a chore if the rider is not in the mood for fast, aggressive riding.

On a track, however, the situation is reversed – the GSX-R's chassis package makes getting the best from the motor very easy indeed. The upside-down Kayaba forks are well-damped, and firmly sprung, while the rear monoshock never shows any hint of fade or overheating. The four-piston Tokico brake calipers work much better than the earlier GSX-R's six-piston items, and wide sticky radial tyres provide immense grip and stability.

Top speed:	274km/h (170mph)
Engine type:	749cc, l/c inline-four, 16-valve, DOHC
Maximum power:	105kW (141bhp) at 12,500rpm
Frame type:	aluminium twin-spar
Tyre sizes:	front 120/70 17, rear 180/55 17
Final drive:	chain
Gearbox:	six-speed
Weight:	166kg (366lb)

Suzuki RF900R

Suzuki's RF900R seemed like a strange machine to launch when it appeared in 1994. The litre-class sportsbike market was dominated by Honda's CBR900RR FireBlade, and Suzuki's own GSX-R1100 was a highly developed sports machine, with massive power from its water-cooled engine. The distinctively styled RF900R with its steel frame and RF600 looks seemed like a distraction from the GSX-R range.

However, when the first bikes appeared in showrooms, riders were immediately won over by the RF900. It had a winning combination of flexible engine power, comfortable riding position, decent handling and capable braking. The 16-valve liquid-cooled engine was all-new, and it produced its 93kW (125bhp) in a very user-friendly manner, with a broad spread of power all the way through the rev range.

The steel beam frame was used to save money over lighter, more sporting aluminium designs, but it is very stiff, and hasn't made the RF too heavy. The braking from the four-piston front brake calipers is impressive, with strong, progressive action. The suspension is rather firm when ridden solo, but with a pillion and a weekend's luggage it begins to work much better. Handling through twisty bends is impressive, with easy, neutral steering, good ground clearance and strong power instantly on tap to pull the rider through the bends.

Used as a fast budget sports tourer, the RF900 will not disappoint. The large dual-seat unit provides comfortable accommodation for two, the wide fairing gives good

weather- and wind-protection and the 21-litre (4.6 gal) fuel tank easily gives 320km
(200 miles) between refuelling stops at touring speeds.

Produced between 1994 and 1999, the RF was a good seller for Suzuki, however
its uncertain identity placed it between two stools. It did not have the
performance to match committed sportsbikes like Honda's CBR900RR or Suzuki's
own GSX-R range, nor the dedicated touring ability of a large-capacity tourer.
Whatever the reasons, the RF was not replaced by an updated model when Suzuki
discontinued it.

Top speed:	264km/h (164mph)
Engine type:	937cc, l/c inline-four, 16-valve, DOHC
Maximum power:	93kW (125bhp) at 10,000rpm
Frame type:	steel twin-spar
Tyre sizes:	front 120/70 17, rear 170/60 17
Final drive:	chain
Gearbox:	six-speed
Weight:	203kg (448lb)

Suzuki GSX-R1000

When Suzuki discontinued its powerful but overweight GSX-R1100 in 1996, the Japanese firm was left without a litre-class sportsbike. Although its GSX-R750 was an excellent machine, it was outclassed in terms of sheer power by Honda's CBR900RR FireBlade, Kawasaki's ZX-9R and the Yamaha R1.

So the only surprise about this 1000cc version of the GSX-R750 was how long it took to appear. Introduced in 2001, the GSX-R1000 instantly went to the top of the performance charts, with the lightest, most powerful engine and chassis package available. Lighter and more powerful than Yamaha's R1, the GSX-R1000 took sportsbike performance to a new level, with a maximum speed of 290km/h (180mph), a 119kW (160bhp) engine and dry weight less than some 600cc bikes.

The GSX-R1000's engine and chassis are both heavily based upon the 2000-model GSX-R750. The aluminium twin-spar frame is identical, except for 0.5mm(0,02in) thicker walls and an extra engine mount, while the swingarm only received minor internal construction modifications.

The engine is the same 16-valve, inline-four layout, with six-speed gearbox and electronic fuel-injection. The cylinder head is the same as the 750, but with a slightly larger combustion chamber, and the overall engine size is only 14mm (0.6in) taller and 6mm (0.2in) longer: both engines are the same width. The fuel-injection is an updated version of the SDTV system first used on the GSX-R750.

As befits a flagship sports model, top-quality suspension units are fitted front and rear. The 43mm (1.7in) Kayaba upside-down front forks are lighter than the GSX-R750 parts, and have a special titanium nitride coating on the stanchions, reducing static friction, or 'stiction'. A piggyback-reservoir rear shock, also by Kayaba, is fully adjustable and gives superb damping on track and road.

The GSX-R1000's front brakes use a pair of Tokico six-piston calipers operating on 320mm (12.6in) discs. These calipers and the gold-coloured fork tubes are the most obvious cosmetic differences between the GSX-R1000 and the GSX-R750.

Top speed:	290km/h (180mph)
Engine type:	988cc, l/c inline-four, 16-valve, DOHC
Maximum power:	119kW (160bhp) at 10,400rpm
Frame type:	aluminium twin-spar
Tyre sizes:	front 120/70 17, rear 190/50 17
Final drive:	chain
Gearbox:	six-speed
Weight:	170kg (375lb)

Suzuki TL1000R

The TL1000R was Suzuki's second attempt at creating a V-twin powered superbike. The TL-R used an updated version of the TL1000S engine, but fitted in a supersports-style track-oriented chassis rather than the half-faired roadbike chassis of the TL-S.

The TL-R has very striking styling – a wide single headlamp fairing incorporates a pair of aggressive ram-air intakes before swooping back in an aerodynamic curve round the aluminium twin-spar frame. The seat unit has a large aerodynamic duck-tail fin, designed to reattach the airflow from the back of the rider, improving high-speed performance.

Under its smooth clothes, the TL-R is a high-specification sports machine. Its engine is the same eight-valve 90° V-twin as fitted to the TL1000S, but with some re-tuning to produce more top-end muscle. It delivers smoother, more linear power than the torquey TL1000S engine, thanks to fuel-injection and timing changes.

But it was the chassis that received most attention from Suzuki's engineers. The TL1000S suffered criticism for its lively handling, and the TL-R is a much more stable ride on the road. A steering damper is fitted as standard, to reduce any tendency for the steering to flap about under hard acceleration, although the revised steering geometry and heavier weight of the TL-R had already added extra stability over the TL1000S design.

The TL-R keeps the same unusual rear suspension system as the TL-S though. The rear spring is mounted separately from the damper unit, and the damper is a unique 'rotary' design. Rather than a conventional linear damper, which pushes a piston through a cylinder of damping oil, the TL damper uses a system of vanes in an oil-filled chamber. The vanes are turned by a shaft linked to the rear swingarm, and the passage of the oil through holes in the vane gives the damping effect.

The brakes were also uprated over the TL1000S, six-piston Tokico calipers replacing the four-piston calipers of the 'S' model.

Top speed:	270km/h (168mph)
Engine type:	996cc, l/c 90° V-twin, eight-valve, DOHC
Maximum power:	101kW (135bhp) at 9500rpm
Frame type:	aluminium twin-spar
Tyre sizes:	front 120/70 17, rear 190/50 17
Final drive:	chain
Gearbox:	six-speed
Weight:	197kg (434lb)

Suzuki TL1000S

The late 1990s saw a rash of new V-twin sports machines, spurred by the success of Ducati's 916. Suzuki's first attempt was the TL1000S, a stylish, half-faired sports machine, with a host of innovative technologies.

The heart of the TL-S is a liquid-cooled V-twin, which produces a healthy 93kW (125bhp) at 9000rpm. Fairing-mounted ram-air intake scoops feed an advanced fuel-injection system which enhances power and reduces emissions, while a slick, six-speed gearbox delivers the power to a broad 190-section rear tyre. The valve-train design is also unusual, using a mixture of chains and gears to drive the camshafts in order to reduce the size of the cylinder heads.

The chassis is unusual. The frame uses an aluminium tube trellis design which combines stiffness with low weight. Upside-down 43mm (1.7in) Kayaba forks are more conventional, but the rear suspension was unique when launched. Rather than use a combined linear spring/damper unit as on most bikes, the TL split the spring from the damper, and used a new rotary damper design. This layout, partly chosen to assist in routing the rear cylinder and exhaust, has been criticized by some experts, although in theory it should offer benefits including reduced friction.

The TL1000S received some criticism for its handling, particularly claims that it was susceptible to front-end instability. Suzuki reacted to these claims by adding a steering damper shortly after the bike was introduced, and retro-fitting the damper

to customers' bikes. The non-adjustable damper fits above the top yoke, and does calm the steering under hard acceleration, although it makes the steering slightly heavier at low speeds.

Despite its strong performance and aggressive character, the TL1000S wasn't a big success for Suzuki. Price discounting did keep sales bouyant in some markets though, and many riders also appreciated the aggressive reputation which the TL had gained through its strong performance and tricky handling. The TL1000S was discontinued in 2002.

Top speed:	257km/h (160mph)
Engine type:	996cc, l/c 90° V-twin, eight-valve, DOHC
Maximum power:	93kW (125bhp) at 9000rpm
Frame type:	aluminium trellis
Tyre sizes:	front 120/70 17, rear 190/50 17
Final drive:	chain
Gearbox:	six-speed
Weight:	187kg (412lb)

Suzuki V-Strom

Suzuki's V-Strom, launched in 2002, is a large-capacity trail-styled tourer based around the V-twin engine from the firm's TL1000. Re-tuned for enhanced low- and mid-range performance, the engine has been updated with the latest version of Suzuki's SDTV dual-valve fuel-injection, and a catalytic converter in the exhaust. Married to an aluminium twin-spar frame with modern, long-travel suspension, the V-Strom (Strom is German for power) follows a conventional design brief for this class of bike. But components like the cast-aluminium wheels, Tarmac-biased tyres and strong roadbike disc brakes tend towards the road part of the trail-style mix. Despite this, the V-Strom is an accomplished tourer.

Top speed:	217km/h (135mph)
Engine type:	996cc, l/c 90° V-twin, eight-valve, DOHC
Maximum power:	73kW (98bhp) at 7600rpm
Frame type:	aluminium twin-spar
Tyre sizes:	front 100/80 19, rear 150/70 17
Final drive:	chain
Gearbox:	six-speed
Weight:	207kg (456lb)

Suzuki GSF1200S Bandit

First launched in 1996, the 1200S Bandit was the half-faired version of Suzuki's 1200cc naked retro machine. Aimed at replicating the sales success of the popular GSF600S Bandit, the big Bandit looked very similar to its smaller-capacity sibling. Following the tried pathway of using parts from existing models to save development costs, the 1200 Bandit used a version of the long-running GSX-R1100 engine, in a simple steel-tube frame. Running gear and ancillaries were borrowed from other machines in Suzuki's lineup, and the 1200 Bandit was an instant success, helped by its competitive price and all-round usability. The half-fairing offered the usual benefits of wind- and weather-protection, also raising the ultimate top speed.

Top speed:	241km/h (150mph)
Engine type:	1157cc, a/c inline-four, 16-valve, DOHC
Maximum power:	75kW (100bhp) at 8500rpm
Frame type:	steel-tube double cradle
Tyre sizes:	front 120/70 17, rear 180/55 17
Final drive:	chain
Gearbox:	five-speed
Weight:	220kg (485lb)

Suzuki GSF1200 Bandit

The GSF1200N Bandit is the unfaired version of Suzuki's budget roadster. Introduced in 1996, its blend of low price, strong engine and retro good looks soon made it popular as an all-rounder. The lack of a fairing put some riders off, since it restricts the long-distance usefulness of the bike, although the naked styling probably attracted almost as many buyers.

The heart of the 1200 Bandit is an air/oil-cooled inline-four engine, based on the 1127cc design used on the GSX-R1100 and GSX1100s of the late 1980s and early 1990s. A 1mm overbore increased the capacity to 1157cc, and other changes reshaped the power curve to improve low-down urge. The Bandit's mid-range is indeed very strong, ideal for a naked street machine such as this. One positive side-effect of using such an old engine is assured reliability – Bandit 1200 engines seldom go wrong.

The Bandit's chassis is completely unremarkable, although effective. Basic, preload-adjustable forks and a preload and rebound-damping adjustable rear monoshock are perfectly suitable for a road bike: ultimate sporting performance is probably restricted by the mediocre ground clearance. The steering is stable and predictable, while the four-piston brakes offer acceptable power and feel.

For the 2000 model year, Suzuki gave the 1200 Bandit a thorough revamp. The changes were most obvious on the faired bike, which got an all-new top fairing, but

the naked Bandit received the same new frame, with a straight steel-tube frame rail running below the fuel tank. This gave a lower seat height and a more stylish look.

The brakes were also heavily revised, with six-piston Tokico calipers replacing the old bike's four-piston parts. Other changes included revised, firmer suspension settings, and useful features such as a new grabrail, and a larger fuel tank.

The 1200 Bandit's cheap price, tough construction and strong engine made it a popular choice for stunt riders in the mid-1990s, and a common sight at stunt shows.

Top speed:	224km/h (140mph)
Engine type:	1157cc, a/c inline-four, 16-valve, DOHC
Maximum power:	75kW (100bhp) at 8500rpm
Frame type:	steel-tube double cradle
Tyre sizes:	front 120/70 17, rear 180/55 17
Final drive:	chain
Gearbox:	five-speed
Weight:	214kg (472lb)

Suzuki GSX1300R Hayabusa

Suzuki's Hayabusa has a rather strange form, but it is one that has been carved by nature. The swooping, bulbous lines of the GSX1300R exist solely to make it perform at high speed – the Hayabusa was the fastest production motorcycle when it was launched in 1999, and has been speed tested at close to 320km/h (200mph).

The 16-valve engine is extremely powerful, despite its conventional design. A multipoint electronic fuel-injection system, and a design based on the GSX-R750, help it produce close to 130kW (180bhp), while remaining comparatively light and compact. The large capacity also means it has a very strong mid-range, as well as massive top-end power. A 'ram-air' intake system uses two inlets either side of the headlight to provide cool, pressurized air to the engine, boosting power as speed increases.

However, it is the bodywork which allows such a high top speed. Drag becomes the defining parameter on performance above 96km/h (60mph), and at 290km/h (180mph)-plus, aerodynamic bodywork is essential. The Hayabusa's large front mudguard, stacked headlight nosecone and large tail unit slice easily through the air.

The Hayabusa is not just a one-dimensional top-speed bike, however. Although heavy and long compared with smaller sports bikes, it has very high-specification suspension, brakes and frame, providing impressively sporting handling. The aluminium frame is immensely strong, and the massive swingarm is braced with stiff

aluminium extrusions and cast sections. Six-piston Tokico brake calipers give ample stopping power, and the 43mm (1.6in) upside-down forks and the rear monoshock are fully adjustable for spring preload, compression and rebound damping. Despite its huge performance, the Hayabusa also makes a sound sports-tourer, with reasonable pillion accommodation and a 275km (170 mile)-plus tank range.

The Hayabusa, which takes its name from a Japanese falcon, was fitted with a 299kph (186mph) speed restrictor in 2001, as part of an attempt to pre-empt statutory speed restrictions on sports machines.

Top speed:	299km/h (186mph)
Engine type:	1298cc, l/c inline-four, 16-valve, DOHC
Maximum power:	130kW (175bhp) at 9800rpm
Frame type:	aluminium twin-spar
Tyre sizes:	front 120/70 17, rear 190/50 17
Final drive:	chain
Gearbox:	six-speed
Weight:	215kg (474lb)

Suzuki GSX1400

Suzuki launched the GSX1400 in 2001 as a response to a market desire for large-capacity naked retro-styled machines. The firm expressed the view that many riders were becoming less interested in ultimate sports machines, because of the twin problems of increasing anti-speeding legislation and tougher insurance premiums.

A handsome machine, the GSX1400 is physically massive – at 228kg (502lb) dry with a 1520mm (60in) wheelbase, it looks every inch the bruising musclebike. Once astride the bike, it still feels extremely wide, but the considerable weight vanishes once on the move.

This muscle-bound image is more than skin-deep. Nestling in a tough steel-tube frame is a brutish lump of an engine – based around the firm's balance-shaft equipped GSX1100 engine from the late 1980s. The 16-valve, DOHC design was a strong, reliable design which has given excellent service, and the increased bore and stroke of the 1402cc update was well within the limits of the tough engine.

Although based on an old air-cooled design, the GSX1400 engine has been updated with a high-tech SDTV dual-throttle fuel-injection system. Borrowed from the GSX-R range of high-tech sports machines, the system uses a computer-controlled secondary throttle valve to match the intake air flow to the engine's demands and the rider's throttle opening.

The GSX1400 engine has been re-tuned for even more low-rpm torque, with a peak figure of 93ft lb at 5000rpm, and is very strong through the mid-range.
The chassis, while conventionally styled, is well-equipped. Six-piston front brake calipers are sportsbike items, while the rear piggyback shocks and 46mm (1.9in) front forks are high-spec, fully adjustable items.

The handling of the GSX is impressive, considering its mass and design. The suspension gives a plush, controlled ride, and although ground clearance is poor for a sportsbike, the GSX is still a very satisfying ride.

Top speed:	241km/h (150mph)
Engine type:	1402cc, a/c inline-four, 16-valve, DOHC
Maximum power:	79kW (106bhp) at 6500rpm
Frame type:	steel-tube double cradle
Tyre sizes:	front 120/70 17, rear 190/50 17
Final drive:	chain
Gearbox:	six-speed
Weight:	228kg (502lb)

Suzuki VL1500 Intruder

The largest-capacity machine in Suzuki's range, the VL1500 is a massive custom-styled cruiser. Dominated by a huge air-cooled V-twin engine, the Intruder is designed for relaxed highway cruising and round-town posing. The engine, with a maximum torque figure of 84ft lb at 2300rpm, is the epitome of the large-capacity, slow-revving engine, although a six-valve design and a front-mounted oil-cooler lend a degree of sophistication. Unusually, the Intruder uses a four-speed gearbox: the broad spread of torque makes more ratios superfluous. Drive to the wide 180-section rear tyre is by clean, maintenance-free shaft drive, and a hidden rear suspension system gives the Intruder the styling of a 'hardtail' custom bike.

Top speed:	280km/h (175mph)
Engine type:	1462cc, a/c 45° V-twin, six-valve, SOHC
Maximum power:	50kW (67bhp) at 2300rpm
Frame type:	steel-tube spine
Tyre sizes:	front 150/80 16, rear 180/70 15
Final drive:	shaft
Gearbox:	four-speed
Weight:	296kg (653lb)

Triumph Speed Four

Triumph's Speed Four is, in part, an attempt to recoup some of the massive investment in developing the TT600 engine and chassis. Essentially a TT600 without the full race fairing, the Speed Four is aimed at the popular middleweight naked bike market. Its aluminium twin-spar frame and liquid-cooled engine are clearly on display, and its high-quality suspension is also retained, giving the highest-spec chassis in the class. The impressive brakes of the TT are also retained. Re-tuning of the TT600 engine has produced a lower peak power output, but improved low-down pull. The Speed Four's styling is borrowed from the firm's Speed Triple. The twin headlamps and small flyscreen echo the bigger bike's 'streetfighter' styling.

Top speed:	224km/h (140mph)
Engine type:	599cc, l/c inline-four, 16-valve, DOHC
Maximum power:	72kW (97bhp) at 11,750rpm
Frame type:	twin-spar aluminium
Tyre sizes:	front 120/70 17, rear 180/55 17
Final drive:	chain
Gearbox:	six-speed
Weight:	170kg (374lb)

Triumph TT600

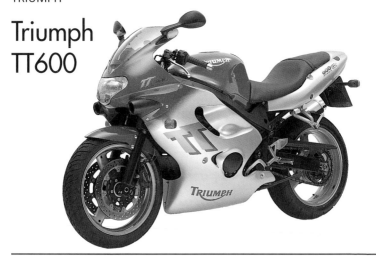

The TT600 was Triumph's first direct assault on a mainstream sector of the motorcycle market. Aimed at providing Triumph with a mass-market middleweight sportsbike, the TT600 had a tough challenge ahead – the 600cc sportsbike class is the most closely contested, and the existing Japanese contenders were intensely well-developed machines.

Triumph followed conventional motorcycle engineering practice with the TT600. A 16-valve, liquid-cooled inline-four engine in an aluminium twin-spar frame is a specification shared with every other bike in this class, although the Sagem fuel-injection was new to the class, and the TT's styling was also unconventional.

As it turned out, both these elements were to work against the TT600. The bulbous fairing was not to everyone's taste, and looked rather dowdy compared with the sharp lines of Yamaha's R6 or Kawasaki's ZX-6R. More seriously, the fuel-injection system was a source of much trouble, with uneven running, poor low-down power and hesitancy.

This was unfortunate, because the TT600's chassis is excellent. The light, stiff frame is fitted with high-spec, fully adjustable Kayaba suspension, lightweight wheels and powerful, progressive Nissin brakes. The light weight is a strong asset, there is excellent ground clearance, and the TT600's track-based development shines through when it is ridden round a circuit.

Peak engine power, while lower than the competition, is still impressive, and the TT also has the benefit of Triumph's excellent build quality. A range of optional factory parts mean the bike can be customized with race exhausts, soft luggage and other accessories.

Triumph has constantly updated the TT600's fuel-injection mapping, and updated engine components have continually improved performance and drivability. The 2002 model was better than ever, although by then much damage had already been done to the TT's reputation.

Top speed:	248km/h (155mph)
Engine type:	599cc, l/c inline-four, 16-valve, DOHC
Maximum power:	80kW (108bhp) at 12,750rpm
Frame type:	twin-spar aluminium
Tyre sizes:	front 120/70 17, rear 180/55 17
Final drive:	chain
Gearbox:	six-speed
Weight:	170kg (374lb)

Triumph Bonneville

An attempt by the Hinckley firm to relive some of Triumph's glory days, the Bonneville is a shameless reincarnation of the famous roadster of the 1960s and 1970s. An all-new engine uses four-valve heads for performance and emissions efficiency, but has been styled externally to look like the OHV design of the old Bonneville. Fake pushrod tubes, rounded cases and a disguised overhead camshaft do a good job – the new 360° twin engine looks very authentic from the outside. Inside, though, it uses a pair of balance shafts to reduce vibration. The rest of the bike follows a similar pattern – modern components with modern performance and reliability, but with 1960s styling.

Top speed:	185km/h (115mph)
Engine type:	790cc, a/c parallel twin, eight-valve, DOHC
Maximum power:	45kW (61bhp) at 7400rpm
Frame type:	steel-tube cradle
Tyre sizes:	front 100/90 19, rear 130/80 17
Final drive:	chain
Gearbox:	five-speed
Weight:	205kg (451lb)

Triumph Bonneville America

The Bonneville America is based on the Bonneville retro roadster but with important mechanical and cosmetic changes. The parallel-twin engine uses a different 270° firing order to give a more syncopated exhaust note from the 360° crank arrangement of the Bonneville. The chassis is also revised, to echo the styling of Triumph's American export models of the past. Feet forward controls, an extra-low seat and pull-back handlebars give an authentic riding position, while the long, low chrome silencers and fat fork shrouds provide proper period styling. Spoked wheels wear fat rubber at the rear, and single disc brakes front and rear afford modern stopping performance. The America offers sedate rather than rapid progress.

Top speed:	177km/h (110mph)
Engine type:	790cc, a/c parallel twin, eight-valve, DOHC
Maximum power:	45kW (61bhp) at 7400rpm
Frame type:	steel-tube cradle
Tyre sizes:	front 110/80 18, rear 170/80 15
Final drive:	chain
Gearbox:	five-speed
Weight:	226kg (497lb)

Triumph Adventurer

As soon as the Thunderbird appeared in 1995, Triumph dealers, especially in America, asked for a custom version. Introduced in 1996, the Adventurer used an almost identical basic engine and chassis package to the Thunderbird, but with a slight cruiser hint to the styling. The 885cc liquid-cooled triple produces 51kW (69bhp), with torquey power delivery. The Triumph steel-tube spine frame works well, while conventional forks and rear monoshock suspension supply soft, plush damping. A 48cm (19in) front wheel and high handlebars give the essential cruiser outline, although the Adventurer is still very much a Triumph in looks and performance. Factory accessories allow extensive customization.

Top speed:	201km/h (125mph)
Engine type:	885cc, l/c inline-triple, 12-valve, DOHC
Maximum power:	51kW (69bhp) at 8000rpm
Frame type:	steel-tube spine
Tyre sizes:	front 100/90 19, rear 150/80 16
Final drive:	chain
Gearbox:	five-speed
Weight:	211kg (465lb)

Triumph Daytona 900

When the reborn Triumph launched its first range of new machines in 1991 and 1992, there were four Daytonas available, 750 and 900 triples, and 1000 and 1200 fours. Launched as a sports model, the Daytonas all had full race twin headlight fairings, adjustable suspension and sporty wheels and tyres. The Daytona 1000 and 750 were not popular, and were discontinued in 1992, but the 900 and 1200 continued up until the late 1990s. The 900 was a particular favourite, its three-cylinder engine combining decent power levels with a characterful sound and torquey delivery. Although it was heavy, and couldn't really compete with advanced Japanese sports machinery, the Daytona was the first in a long line of sporting Triumphs.

Top speed:	241km/h (150mph)
Engine type:	885cc, l/c inline-triple, 12-valve, DOHC
Maximum power:	73kW (98bhp) at 9000rpm
Frame type:	steel-tube spine
Tyre sizes:	front 120/70 17, rear 180/55 17
Final drive:	chain
Gearbox:	six-speed
Weight:	216kg (476lb)

Triumph Legend

Essentially a budget version of the Thunderbird, the Legend was introduced in 1998 in two versions. The basic Legend TT had 43cm (17in) wire-spoked wheels and an extra-low seat height. The Legend Deluxe had an even lower seat, and came with two-tone paintwork. Both bikes shared the 885cc liquid-cooled triple engine of the Thunderbird, its 51kW (69bhp) and torquey power delivery giving relatively sprightly performance. Cost cutting (the Legend was almost $2,000 [$3,200] cheaper than the Thunderbird) is hard to spot on the Legend, and it offers good value for an entry-level machine. Triumph's strong build quality and finish are continued on these models, and both engine and chassis are almost identical to the Thunderbird.

Top speed:	201km/h (125mph)
Engine type:	885cc, l/c inline-triple, 12-valve, DOHC
Maximum power:	51kW (69bhp) at 8000rpm
Frame type:	steel-tube spine
Tyre sizes:	front 110/80 18, rear 150/80 16
Final drive:	chain
Gearbox:	six-speed
Weight:	220kg (485lb)

Triumph Thunderbird

Based around the company's 885cc inline-triple engine, the Thunderbird combines modern Hinckley Triumph performance and engineering with the simple good looks of the previous generation of Triumphs. Installed in a low-slung retro chassis, the liquid-cooled engine looks superb, with its chromed casings and fake air-cooling fins. Matching the retro styling are a pair of 'peashooter' silencers and rubber kneepads on the tank. A choice of two-tone colour schemes, wire-spoked wheels and a single brake disc front and rear round off the design nicely, although the brakes need a firm squeeze to stop quickly. The Thunderbird makes a relaxing alternative to cruisers like Harley's Dyna Glide or Yamaha's Drag Star. Engine reliability is exemplary.

Top speed:	201km/h (125mph)
Engine type:	885cc, l/c inline-triple, 12-valve, DOHC
Maximum power:	51kW (69bhp) at 8000rpm
Frame type:	steel-tube spine
Tyre sizes:	front 110/80 18, rear 150/80 16
Final drive:	chain
Gearbox:	six-speed
Weight:	220kg (485lb)

Triumph Thunderbird Sport

The Thunderbird Sport is a revised update of the basic Thunderbird, with similar retro styling, although the design is from a 1970s dirt-track styled racer. Dominated by stylish upswept twin silencers on the right hand side, it has a fine blend of styling and performance. The engine is little changed from the basic Thunderbird, and still produces a torquey 51kW (69bhp), driving through a six-speed gearbox. The suspension is fully adjustable at both ends, and the spoked wheels have wider 43cm (17in) rims which can be fitted with modern sports tyres. The brakes let the Sport down though – the two twin piston calipers up front lack outright power. The Sport has a pillion seat, but is at its happiest when ridden solo.

Top speed:	209km/h (130mph)
Engine type:	885cc, l/c inline-triple, 12-valve, DOHC
Maximum power:	51kW (69bhp) at 8000rpm
Frame type:	steel-tube spine
Tyre sizes:	front 120/70 17, rear 160/60 17
Final drive:	chain
Gearbox:	six-speed
Weight:	224kg (493lb)

Triumph Trophy 900

The Trophy 900 is a smaller capacity version of the firm's 1200 Trophy tourer, and looks externally similar. A large touring fairing with tall windscreen and full weather-protection is wrapped round one of Hinckley Triumph's oldest frame and engine designs. The steel-tube spine frame was the original 'modular' frame fitted to almost all of the first generation of new Triumphs in 1991, and the 885cc triple engine is just as old. Both chassis and engine are eminently suitable for this touring role, although a shaft final drive would have extended the Trophy's usefulness. Hard luggage as standard and a large fuel tank underline the Trophy's usability though; it can go as far as is needed, in speed and comfort.

Top speed:	217km/h (135mph)
Engine type:	885cc, l/c inline-triple, 12-valve, DOHC
Maximum power:	73kW (98bhp) at 9000rpm
Frame type:	steel-tube spine
Tyre sizes:	front 120/70 17, rear 170/60 17
Final drive:	chain
Gearbox:	six-speed
Weight:	220kg (485lb)

Triumph Daytona 955i

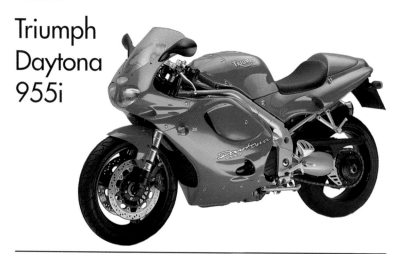

The Daytona has always been Triumph's flagship sportsbike, so when the firm launched a new-generation sportsbike in 1997 it simply had to take that name. First unveiled as the T595 Daytona, the new bike had a very impressive spec, and was aimed at taking on the might of the Japanese top-class sportsbikes, such as Honda's FireBlade and Kawasaki's ZX-9R.

The heart of the original T595 was an uprated 955cc triple engine, based on the earlier three-cylinder designs. Fitted with an advanced fuel-injection system designed by the French firm Sagem, the engine produced a remarkable peak power figure of 97kW (130bhp), together with the trademark torquey mid-range and soulful sound of the inline three-cylinder design.

The chassis was also rather remarkable. An aluminium tubed perimeter frame design was chosen to combine stiffness and low weight, while looking different from the usual Japanese twin-spar aluminium frames. Mated to an elegant single-sided rear swingarm and stiff, 45mm (1.8in) fully adjustable front forks, the T595 chassis was every bit as accomplished as its engine.

Although the T595 couldn't get the better of the Japanese – Yamaha's R1 appeared nine months later, redefining sporting motorcycles – it was still a successful model, combining Triumph character and heritage with genuinely sporting performance.

The 1998 model year saw a renaming of the T595 as the Daytona 955i. Cosmetic changes were made, as well as a redesigned exhaust to improve ground clearance.

But it wasn't until the 2001 update that significant changes were made to the Daytona. This latest version reverted to a double-sided swingarm to reduce weight and improve stiffness, and new bodywork sharpened the styling of the Daytona. Extensive engine upgrades produced another power increase, this time to a very impressive 110kW (147bhp). And while the opposition has moved on in terms of track performance, the latest Daytona makes an impressive sporting machine for road use.

Top speed:	272k,/h (170mph)
Engine type:	955cc, l/c inline-triple, 12-valve, DOHC
Maximum power:	110kW (147bhp) at 10,700rpm
Frame type:	aluminium tube perimeter
Tyre sizes:	front 120/70 17, rear 180/55 17
Final drive:	chain
Gearbox:	six-speed
Weight:	188kg (414lb)

Triumph
Speed Triple

This latest incarnation of the Speed Triple is Triumph's best yet. Using the frame and engine from its flagship Daytona sportsbike, Triumph has created a naked musclebike which offers strong performance and quirky looks.

The first Speed Triple appeared in 1994, using the 885cc triple engine from the first Daytona 900 in a steel-tube spine frame with a single round headlight. Performance was brisk, the torquey engine producing 73kW (98bhp), and the Daytona-derived chassis allowed nimble handling.

For 1997, the Triple was updated, and renamed the Speed Triple T509. The 885cc engine received Sagem fuel-injection, and the steel-tube frame was replaced with a new aluminium tube perimeter frame and single-sided swingarm, again borrowed from Triumph's flagship sportsbike, the T595 Daytona. Peak power also increased, this time to 80kW (108bhp).

This pattern of following the development of the Daytona continued for 1998 and 2002 model years. The latest Speed Triple has the most recent 955i Daytona engine, producing 88kW (118bhp), with a strong, torquey delivery. Visually similar to the 1998 bike, the 2002 Triple had a host of internal engine mods, including raised compression, larger valves and new pistons.

Revised airbox and exhaust characteristics further improved power delivery.

The sportsbike-quality chassis gives the 2002 Triple outstanding handling, although the sharp steering geometry, together with a short wheelbase and powerful engine can make the Speed Triple feel quite lively over bumps. The suspension is also rather firm for bumpy road comfort, although the brakes are very impressive, stopping the Triple quickly and accurately from speed.

Kept around town or on mountain backroads, the Speed Triple is an impressive performer, which can surprise sportsbike riders on the track, where its good ground clearance, firm suspension and splendid brakes are all at home.

Top speed:	240km/h (50mph)
Engine type:	955cc, l/c inline-triple, 12-valve, DOHC
Maximum power:	88kW (118bhp) at 9100rpm
Frame type:	aluminium tube perimeter
Tyre sizes:	front 120/70 17, rear 190/50 17
Final drive:	chain
Gearbox:	six-speed
Weight:	189kg (416lb)

Triumph Sprint RS

The Sprint RS is a half-faired variant of the Sprint ST sports tourer. Cheaper than the ST, it is aimed at riders who want a sportier ride than the ST, but with the good road manners of the Sprint chassis and engine. The chassis is largely the same as the ST, with the exception of the swingarm: the RS wears a cheaper, lighter double-sided swingarm rather than the ST's single-sided item. This change, and with less bodywork, gives the RS a hefty 8kg (18lb) weight advantage over its sibling. Suspension and brakes are unchanged from the ST. The latest 2002 version of the RS is fitted with the same 955cc engine as the Speed Triple and the ST. The three-cylinder engine is a refined, well-developed powerplant with plenty of power and torque.

Top speed:	248km/h (155mph)
Engine type:	955cc, l/c inline-triple, 12-valve, DOHC
Maximum power:	88kW (118bhp) at 9100rpm
Frame type:	twin-spar aluminium
Tyre sizes:	front 120/70 17, rear 180/55 17
Final drive:	chain
Gearbox:	six-speed
Weight:	199kg (438lb)

Triumph Sprint ST

First unveiled at the end of 1998, Triumph's Sprint ST is the Hinckley firm's interpretation of the modern sports-tourer bike. Long dominated by Honda's VFR800, this competitive sector of the market requires a machine with the comfort for easy 1200km (750-mile) days, as well as track-friendly performance on arrival. On paper, the Sprint ST fits the bill. Powered by Triumph's latest 955cc three-cylinder engine, the ST can hit 256km/h (160mph), while weighing less than the VFR, at just 207kg (456lb). Adjustable suspension and sporty tyres add chassis sporting potential, and the sleek bodywork and single-sided swingarm supply classic good looks. Strong, sportsbike brakes give class-leading performance.

Top speed:	256km/h (160mph)
Engine type:	955cc, l/c inline-triple, 12-valve, DOHC
Maximum power:	88kW (118bhp) at 9100rpm
Frame type:	twin-spar aluminium
Tyre sizes:	front 120/70 17, rear 180/55 17
Final drive:	chain
Gearbox:	six-speed
Weight:	207kg (456lb)

Triumph Tiger 955i

Triumph's trail-styled Tiger has long been one of the firm's most successful and popular models, especially in continental European countries like Germany. Originally introduced in 1992, as one of the first new-generation Hinckley Triumphs, the first Tiger used the carburetted 885cc triple engine shared with the Daytona, Trophy and Trident models.

The high-output 12-valve engine was mated to a tough steel-tube cradle frame, fitted with long-travel dirtbike-type suspension at both ends. Wire-spoked wheels, knobbly off-road tyres and a small twin headlamp half-fairing completed the Tiger's styling.

But, like most large-capacity trail-styled bikes, the big, heavy Tiger was completely unsuitable for off-road use. However, the massive weight, strong power and fragile bodywork which ruled out off-road work made the Tiger an excellent road bike, which was especially at home carrying out two-up touring duties on the autobahns and motorways of Europe.

In 1999, a revised Tiger was introduced, with an updated, fuel-injected engine, improved running gear and sleek, modern bodywork. Despite more compact styling, the new Tiger was slightly heavier, although the engine's increased power outweighed any performance deficit. A new steel perimeter frame and more refined suspension front and rear gave stiffer handling, and improved equipment levels made the Tiger even more suited to long-distance touring rides.

The latest 2001 update makes the Tiger one of the most powerful trail-styled bikes available. Triumph fitted the revamped 955cc triple engine from the Daytona 955i, and its torque figure of 67ft lb means strong, smooth acceleration from low down in the rev range. The Sagem fuel-injection is glitch-free and gives superb carburation all the way through the rev range, as well as impressive economy.

A large 24-litre (5.3 gal) fuel tank permits a fuel range easily in excess of 320km (200 miles), and official Triumph accessories like hard luggage, electrically heated grips and taller screens further enhance the Tiger's touring credentials.

Top speed:	216km/h (135mph)
Engine type:	955cc, l/c inline-triple, 12-valve, DOHC
Maximum power:	76kW (104bhp) at 9500rpm
Frame type:	steel-tube perimeter
Tyre sizes:	front 110/80 19, rear 150/70 17
Final drive:	chain
Gearbox:	six-speed
Weight:	215kg (474lb)

Triumph Trophy 1200

Triumph's Trophy 1200 is a heavyweight tourer based around the firm's 1180cc inline-four 16-valve engine. The Trophy is one of Triumph's earliest Hinckley models, and a strong, reliable design. Updates in 1995 and 1998 were mostly cosmetic, the basic bike needing little modification. The Trophy slots its strong engine into a full touring chassis, with a steel-tube spine frame, large fairing and hard luggage, while its 25-litre (5.5 gal) fuel tank allows over 320km (200 miles) between refills. Conventional, softly sprung suspension gives a plush ride, although the top-heavy frame design makes the Trophy feel ungainly at low speeds. The Trophy is a fine tourer, but dedicated high-mileage fans will be disappointed at the lack of shaft drive.

Top speed:	224km/h (140mph)
Engine type:	1180cc, l/c inline-four, 16-valve, DOHC
Maximum power:	80kW (107bhp) at 9000rpm
Frame type:	steel-tube spine
Tyre sizes:	front 120/70 17, rear 170/60 17
Final drive:	chain
Gearbox:	six-speed
Weight:	235kg (518lb)

Victory
V92C Cruiser

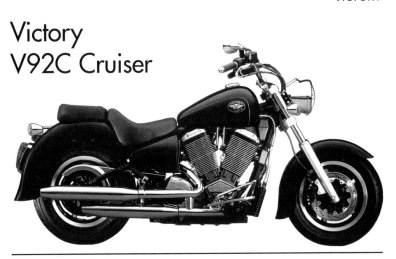

Produced by the American Polaris snowmobile company, the Victory V92 was launched in 2000 as an alternative to the hegemony of Harley-Davidson in the US cruiser market. A conventionally styled cruiser in many ways, the V92 is nevertheless an advanced, well-designed machine. The air-cooled engine has four valves per cylinder, two chain-driven overhead camshafts and complex fuel-injection. It produces a strong, torquey power delivery, peaking at 46kW (62bhp) at 4500rpm. The cruiser chassis is accomplished enough for cruising duties, while the styling is pure US custom, with twin staggered chrome exhausts and extensive chrome plate. Advanced electronic instruments include a clock and diagnostic display.

Top speed:	177km/h (110mph)
Engine type:	1507cc, a/c 50° V-twin, eight-valve, SOHC
Maximum power:	46kW (62bhp) at 4500rpm
Frame type:	steel-tube double cradle
Tyre sizes:	front 90/90 16, rear 160/80 16
Final drive:	belt
Gearbox:	five-speed
Weight:	286kg (630lb)

Victory V92SC Sport Cruiser

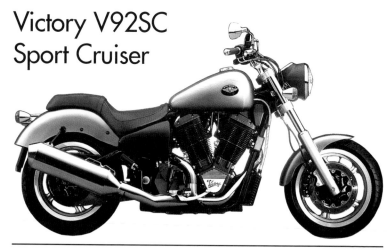

The Victory motorcycle company is owned by Polaris, an American snowmobile manufacturer. The Sport Cruiser is based on the firm's V92 Cruiser, so it shares the 1507cc fuel-injected V-twin engine of the cruiser, although the SC produces 7.5kW (10bhp) more, thanks to a two-into-one exhaust system. The frame is similar, but the Sport Cruiser has much higher-spec chassis components. The wheels are sportsbike-style 43cm (17in) cast items, fitted with sports radial tyres. Brakes are upgraded with twin discs at the front, and the suspension is also more refined, with massive 50mm (2in) Marzocchi forks and a Fox rear monoshock. Though a satisfying ride, the V92SC has insufficient ground clearance for sportier riding.

Top speed:	177km/h (110mph)
Engine type:	1507cc, a/c 50° V-twin, eight-valve, SOHC
Maximum power:	54kW (72bhp) at 4750rpm
Frame type:	steel-tube double cradle
Tyre sizes:	front 120/70 17, rear 180/55 17
Final drive:	belt
Gearbox:	five-speed
Weight:	286kg (630lb)

Yamaha T-Max

The European scooter market is vital for many manufacturers, and demand for larger-capacity machines grew throughout the 1990s. Yamaha's T-Max was the biggest capacity scooter available when it was launched in 2000, but was soon overtaken by Honda's 600cc Silver Wing. The T-Max uses a parallel twin engine laid down under the scooter's footboards. A separate swingarm arrangement uses an automatic belt drive system to provide 'twist and go' riding. Top speed is over 160km/h (100mph), while a six-second 0–60mph (96km/h) time beats many sports cars. The chassis offers secure, accomplished handling – the steel-tube frame is stiff, disc brakes are strong and well-damped suspension front and rear allows sporty riding.

Top speed:	168km/h (105mph)
Engine type:	499cc, l/c parallel twin, eight-valve, DOHC
Maximum power:	30kW (40bhp) at 7000rpm
Frame type:	steel-tube space frame
Tyre sizes:	front 120/70 14, rear 150/70 14
Final drive:	belt
Gearbox:	automatic
Weight:	197kg (433lb)

Yamaha
FZS600 Fazer

Yamaha's Fazer looked like a straightforward budget offering when it first appeared in 1997. Styled like the Japanese-market Fazer 400, the Fazer 600 used a re-tuned version of the Thundercat engine, in a steel-tube frame. But the high-performance front brake calipers – shared with the R1 superbike – and aluminium monoshock rear suspension hinted at sportier performance than the likes of Suzuki's Bandit 600, the budget 600 market leader at the time.

On the road, the Fazer is an excellent performer. The 599cc engine is fitted with smaller carburettors than on the Thundercat, providing the Fazer with superior low-down and mid-range torque for effortless, fast progress. The maximum speed of around 232km/h (145mph) quickly appears, but it is the friendly, easy delivery of the power that most impresses.

The basic but capable chassis blends remarkable sporting prowess with the comfort and usability of a long-distance machine, while the brakes provide the best performance in its class, by a long chalk. Power, feel and progression are all present, and the Fazer's low weight makes the brakes even more impressive.

Unlike the Bandit or Hornet, the Fazer comes only as a half-faired model. The small twin headlight unit provides impressive wind- and weather-protection, although its styling wasn't initially to everyone's taste, and the headlights performed rather poorly at night.

For 2000, the Fazer received a minor update, in the shape of a larger-capacity fuel tank, up 2 litres (0.4 gal) to 20 litres (4.4 gal), while the dash received a new digital clock and the forks gained preload adjusters. The extra tank capacity further improved the already impressive range, making the Fazer even more user-friendly.

In 2002, the Fazer saw a more significant revision. A new fairing, based around the FZS1000 Fazer 1000 design updated its styling and markedly improved headlight performance. The tank also received another capacity increase to 22 litres (4.8 gal): easily enough for 320km (200 miles) between fill-ups.

Top speed:	232km/h (145mph)
Engine type:	599cc, l/c inline-four, 16-valve, DOHC
Maximum power:	71kW (95bhp) at 11,500rpm
Frame type:	steel-tube double cradle
Tyre sizes:	front 110/70 17, rear 160/60 17
Final drive:	chain
Gearbox:	six-speed
Weight:	188kg (414lb)

Yamaha YZF600R Thundercat

Like many bikes, Yamaha's Thundercat was initially launched as a sports machine, but has remained successful in a different, sport-touring role after being superseded by more advanced designs. First seen in 1996, the Thundercat replaced the elderly FZR600R and was an immediate success. Its inline-four engine was based on the FZR, but heavily revised for improved power and torque. The frame was also similar to the FZR, using a steel Deltabox design, together with an aluminium swingarm. The result was a bike that was heavier and less focused than its predecessor, but with more modern performance.

The styling is very distinctive. The aerodynamic single headlight nosecone is similar to the Thunderace 1000, also launched in 1996, and incorporates a ram-air induction system which increases the engine's output as speed increases. Also shared with the Thunderace are the four piston front brake calipers, manufactured by Sumitomo and shared with many recent Yamaha models. These brakes, which were a revelation to many riders in 1996, are still among the best performing brake components on the road.

The conventional suspension setup is soft for a sportsbike, but is still capable on road and track. Many 600 Supersports racers campaigned the Thundercat, with remarkable success, including at world level (Vittoriano Guareschi finished second on a Thundercat in the 1997 WSS championship). The suspension's built-in adjustment front and rear can improve performance, but aftermarket

improvements can pay dividends for track use.

Equipment levels are sufficient rather than extensive, and the Thundercat's sports-derived dashboard is less comprehensive than some all-round competitors. Having said that, its 19-litre (4.2 gal) fuel tank gives an extended range, and the spacious dual seat offers comfort for many miles.

The Thundercat has received only minor changes during its life so far, suggesting Yamaha got the design largely right to begin with.

Top speed:	257km/h (160mph)
Engine type:	599cc, l/c inline-four, 16-valve, DOHC
Maximum power:	75kW (100bhp) at 11,500rpm
Frame type:	Deltabox steel twin-spar
Tyre sizes:	front 120/60 17, rear 160/60 17
Final drive:	chain
Gearbox:	six-speed
Weight:	187kg (411lb)

Yamaha YZF-R6

By 1999, Yamaha's Thundercat had already been relegated to fourth place in the sports 600 market: Kawasaki's ZX-6R and Suzuki's GSX-R600 were both better performers, especially on track, while Honda's CBR600 was the better all-round performer.

Luckily for Yamaha, it had a replacement waiting in the wings. The firm's R1 had taken the litre-class sportsbike world by storm the year before, and its new R6 used many similar design concepts to similar good effect.

The R6's all-new engine was a conventional 16-valve inline-four layout, although it used the double-split crankcases of the R1. This allows the gearbox input and output shafts to be 'stacked' one above the other, giving a shorter, more compact engine design. A bold, central air intake in the sharp top fairing leads to a pressurized 'ram-air' box which feeds the engine with cool, dense air through four 37mm (1.5in) Keihin carburettors.

Like the engine, the chassis uses well-developed conventional technologies and design rather than revolutionary techniques. The twin-spar aluminium frame is very short and stiff, and while the aluminium swingarm is longer than normal for improved roadholding, the monoshock rear suspension and right-way-up front forks are standard road bike parts. Although the front brakes give class-leading performance, they are the same Sumitomo calipers used on the Thundercat.

On the road, the R6's performance is manic. The powerful engine redlines at 15,500rpm, and is best kept above 8000 revs for best progress. There's a step in the power curve here, and another around 11,000rpm, above which the really strong power lives. The short, sharp chassis is a joy on twisty roads, although the suspension is a bit soft for really intense track riding.

For 2001, the R6 received a minor update, with a new sleeker tail unit that incorporated a lightweight, low-maintenance LED rear light, a first on a production motorcycle.

Top speed:	264km/h (164mph)
Engine type:	600cc, l/c inline-four, 16-valve, DOHC
Maximum power:	89kW (120bhp) at 13,000rpm
Frame type:	aluminium twin-spar
Tyre sizes:	front 120/60 17, rear 180/55 17
Final drive:	chain
Gearbox:	six-speed
Weight:	168kg (370lb)

Yamaha XVS650 Drag Star

Yamaha has always had a strong presence in the middleweight cruiser market, and this 650 Drag Star, introduced in 1997, had to fill the classily chromed shoes of the firm's successful, long-running XV535 Virago.

The Drag Star uses a larger-capacity version of the well-proven Virago engine, but in a 'lowrider'-styled chassis. The imitation hardtail rear monoshock suspension and brushed fork shrouds, together with the tank-mounted speedometer and deep valanced mudguards, give the Drag Star typical cruiser good looks.

Many parts are chrome-plated, including the exhaust, headlight and engine casings, and the wide, spoked rear-wheel looks suitably authentic.

The simple air-cooled engine uses a SOHC valve-train and two-valve cylinder heads, with twin Mikuni carburettors. Using a larger bore and stroke than the 535 donor engine, it drives through a wet clutch to a five-speed gearbox, and clean, low-maintenance shaft drive ensures trouble-free final drive.

Performance is brisk enough for a medium-capacity cruiser. The willing engine's 30kW (40bhp) appears in a satisfyingly torquey manner, and the capable chassis performs well to the limits of its ground clearance. The single front brake disc with a two-piston sliding caliper looks underwhelming, but together with the strong rear drum brake provides excellent stopping ability.

The Drag Star is no performance machine, however, and is best kept for light summer cruises, although its economic performance and shaft drive make it a stylish alternative for commuting duties.

The low-slung seat height of just 695mm (27in) is ideal for shorter riders, while wide pullback bars and forward foot controls make for a comfortable riding position.

There is a massive choice of aftermarket accessories for the Drag Star, including chromed parts, cissy bars, screens and luggage.

Top speed:	161km/h (100mph)
Engine type:	649cc, a/c 75° V-twin, four-valve, SOHC
Maximum power:	30kW (40bhp) at 6500rpm
Frame type:	steel-tube double cradle
Tyre sizes:	front 110/90 19, rear 170/80 15
Final drive:	shaft
Gearbox:	five-speed
Weight:	215kg (474lb)

Yamaha YZF-R7

Yamaha had already introduced the R1 and the R6 in 1998, so there was little surprise when it also announced the R7, a 750cc member of the new 'R' series.

But the R7 was very different from the other two bikes. While the R1 and R6 were mass-production road vehicles, designed to be sold in their thousands to the riding public worldwide, the R7 was a limited-edition racebike. The requirements of World Superbike racing meant Yamaha had to build and sell a certain number of machines to the public to make its new bike eligible.

The R7 was not cheap, costing almost £22,000 ($35,000) when launched in the UK.

Ironically, that money didn't buy an awful lot of performance. Yamaha only built one model for sale, which had to comply with worldwide road-going homologation rules. So power limits in countries like France and Switzerland meant the bike could only produce around 75kW (100bhp) – much less than the R1 which cost less than half as much.

But it is for the track that the R7 was really produced, and with the Yamaha race kit installed it produces much more power, closer to 119kW (160bhp). The R7 engine used the same design techniques as the R1, so it had a 20-valve head, double split crankcases and a stacked gearbox. However, the R7 uses much more exotic materials, including titanium valves and conrods.

The advanced fuel-injection system has two injectors per cylinder, although only one fires as standard – the ECU computer provided in the official Yamaha race kit allows the second injector to operate.

The rest of the design is conventional, but extremely high quality. The black-finished frame and swingarm are aluminium Deltabox designs, and combine extreme stiffness with low weight. Öhlins suspension front and rear is full factory race quality, and although the brakes are the same as fitted to the R1 and R6, they still offer amazing performance.

Top speed:	298km/h (185mph)
Engine type:	749cc, l/c inline-four, 20-valve, DOHC
Maximum power:	119kW (160bhp) at 11,000rpm
Frame type:	aluminium twin-spar
Tyre sizes:	front 120/70 17, rear 180/55 17
Final drive:	chain
Gearbox:	six-speed
Weight:	176kg (388lb)

Yamaha TDM850

Yamaha's TDM850 was a street-biased variant on the many 'dual sport' on/off-road machines launched in the late 1980s. It used a big bore engine from the firm's 750cc Super Tenere trailbike, in a steel twin-spar Deltabox chassis, with road wheels and tyres and long-travel suspension. The parallel twin engine offers rather uninspiring performance, although it has decent power for an 850 twin. There is no appreciable step in the power, and the TDM can feel rather bland. The post-1996 model was better – Yamaha modified the engine's firing order with a 270º crankshaft to give a lumpier feel. Many owners criticized the TDM's gearbox for poor gear ratios and excessive snatch, although the five-speed box keeps changes to a minimum.

Top speed:	208km/h (129mph)
Engine type:	849cc, l/c parallel twin, 10-valve, DOHC
Maximum power:	60kW (80bhp) at 7500rpm
Frame type:	steel twin-spar
Tyre sizes:	front 110/80 18, rear 150/70 17
Final drive:	chain
Gearbox:	five-speed
Weight:	201kg (443lb)

Yamaha TRX850

The TRX850 was an attempt to cash in on the success of European-style sports twins, especially in the Japanese home market. Following enthusiastic reviews in Japan, it was introduced to Europe in 1996, where it sold steadily. The TRX used a new version of the TDM850 engine in a steel-tube trellis frame with sportsbike suspension and half-fairing. The parallel twin engine received an altered firing order, with a new 270° crankshaft intended to give the TRX the syncopated sound and character of a V-twin design. It is not a massively powerful motor, producing just 59kW (79bhp), but is sufficient for a middleweight sports twin. The chassis is rather low-tech in places though, and doesn't have the class of the Italian designs it echoes.

Top speed:	233km/h (145mph)
Engine type:	849cc, l/c parallel twin, 10-valve, DOHC
Maximum power:	59kW (79bhp) at 7250rpm
Frame type:	steel-tube trellis
Tyre sizes:	front 120/60 17, rear 160/60 17
Final drive:	chain
Gearbox:	five-speed
Weight:	190kg (418lb)

Yamaha TDM900

Cosmetically similar to the TDM850, the TDM900 is nevertheless a wheels-up revamp of the earlier bike. Based on the same design concept as the original, the 900 gave Yamaha a chance to update the TDM's specification. So while the frame looks similar to the old bike, it is made of aluminium rather than steel, and the engine uses modern internals, including ceramic-coated bores, but is broadly similar to the old motor. Other changes include a new fuel-injection system. From the rider's seat, the TDM has an updated dash, but the rest of the bike feels similar to the older machine. The engine offers torquey progress, but is flat compared to some competing designs. The chassis works well though, and the front brakes are superb.

Top speed:	225km/h (140mph)
Engine type:	897cc, l/c parallel twin, 10-valve, DOHC
Maximum power:	64kW (86bhp) at 7500rpm
Frame type:	aluminium twin-spar
Tyre sizes:	front 120/70 18, rear 160/60 17
Final drive:	chain
Gearbox:	six-speed
Weight:	190kg (419lb)

Yamaha XJ900 Diversion

Not Yamaha's most glamorous model, the XJ900 Diversion is nevertheless a long-running, popular bike. First introduced to replace the XJ900 in 1994, it is an excellent budget tourer. The 892cc air-cooled engine is dated, but has proved its economy and reliability since first appearing in the 1985 XJ900. The eight-valve design is strong at the bottom end of the rev range, but quickly runs out of go at higher speeds. A five-speed gearbox provides well-spaced ratios for relaxed touring progress, and the smooth shaft final drive is virtually maintenance-free. The 900 Diversion's frame-mounted half-fairing and tall screen give good weather-protection, and a roomy dual seat allows many miles to be covered two-up in comfort.

Top speed:	206km/h (128mph)
Engine type:	892cc, a/c inline-four, eight-valve, DOHC
Maximum power:	67kW (90bhp) at 8250rpm
Frame type:	steel-tube double cradle
Tyre sizes:	front 120/70 17, rear 180/55 17
Final drive:	shaft
Gearbox:	five-speed
Weight:	239kg (527lb)

Yamaha FZR1000

The original FZR1000 Genesis appeared in 1988, when its liquid-cooled 20-valve engine (based on the FZ750 engine) and aluminium twin-spar frame were right at the cutting edge of motorcycle engineering. It was an instant success, and was updated the following year to produce the FZR1000 EXUP, which remained at the top of the sportsbike class until Honda's CBR900RR FireBlade appeared in 1992.

The EXUP, as the FZR became known, combined a very powerful 93kW (125bhp)-plus engine with an accomplished sports chassis. EXUP (Exhaust Ultimate Powervalve) refers to an electrically operated valve in the exhaust system which alters the flow characteristics in the downpipes to suit different rev ranges.

The FZR's five-valve layout is also a trademark Yamaha design, first seen on the FZ750. Three inlet valves and two exhaust valves allow high-rpm breathing and an efficient combustion chamber shape. The result of these technologies is an engine which combines strong mid-range power with a large peak-horsepower figure.

The last version of the EXUP, the 1995 RU model, was the most refined, featuring Öhlins upside-down front forks and six-piston front brake calipers. A cosmetic revamp in 1994 replaced the earlier projector-beam headlights with a pair of stylish fox-eye lamps, and although some of the later colour schemes were a bit garish for some tastes, the last EXUP is a good-looking machine.

The riding position is a no-nonsense sports-style, with a long stretch over the tank to the low handlebars, and while this helps the rider tuck into a racing crouch at high speeds, it's not the most comfortable position for long distances. The dual seat is rather meagre for two-up touring too, although the FZR has both the engine performance and 240km (150 mile)-plus tank range required for long, fast trips.

The EXUP's engine design still lives on, despite the FZR beign discontinued in 1996. Yamaha's Thunderace uses basically the same motor in a 108kW (145bhp) form to power its sport-touring chassis.

Top speed:	275km/h (171mph)
Engine type:	1002cc, inline-four, 20-valve, DOHC
Maximum power:	93kW (125bhp) at 10,000rpm
Frame type:	aluminium twin-spar
Tyre sizes:	front 120/70 17, rear 180/55 17
Final drive:	chain
Gearbox:	five-speed
Weight:	209kg (461lb)

Yamaha FZS1000 Fazer

From the moment the Fazer 600 first appeared in 1997, many riders asked for a large-capacity version of the versatile all-rounder. It took Yamaha four years, until 2001, to introduce such a bike, the Fazer 1000. Clearly built with a similar design brief to the Fazer 600, the bigger Fazer is a capable, high-quality all-round sporting machine, based around the R1 engine.

The 998cc engine is slightly changed from its supersports origins, but retains almost all its massively strong power. The cylinder head is modified to accept sidedraught carburettors, and the clutch is smaller and more compact. The new carburettors are smaller than the R1 parts, improving low-down power without losing too much at the top end. There is an abundance of power throughout the rev range, Yamaha's EXUP valve system boosting mid-range power, and a free-flowing four-into-one stainless-steel exhaust system helping the impressive top end.

This hugely capable engine is fitted into a simple yet effective steel frame, mounted on quality, adjustable suspension at both ends. The 43mm (1.7in) front forks and piggyback rear shock are soft as standard, but provide excellent damping and springing for the road. On a racetrack, they will need to be adjusted, but the road bias of the Fazer 1000 will also show on track in its average ground clearance.

But the Fazer 1000 is not designed as a track machine. Rather it is an all-round versatile sportsbike for the road, that combines a comfortable seat, small wind-

cheating half-fairing and comprehensive instrumentation, with outstanding R1-type brakes and a 266km/h (165mph) maximum speed. It's as comfortable on long two-up touring trips as on backroad scratching sessions and day-to-day commuting duties. However, the biggest handicap to sales success was the Fazer's high price – it cost over £8,000 (\$12,800) when it was launched in the UK.

Yamaha did slightly spoil the performance of the Fazer by fitting dated Metzeler sport-touring tyres, rather than a more modern tyre. Sporting riders are advised to swap these at the first opportunity for grippier rubber.

Top speed:	266km/h (165mph)
Engine type:	998cc, l/c inline-four, 20-valve, DOHC
Maximum power:	107kW (143bhp) at 10,000rpm
Frame type:	steel-tube double cradle
Tyre sizes:	front 120/70 17, rear 180/55 17
Final drive:	chain
Gearbox:	six-speed
Weight:	208kg (459lb)

Yamaha YZF1000 Thunderace

In 1996, when the Thunderace was released, the litre-class sportsbike sector had been dominated by one bike – Honda's FireBlade – for four years. Yamaha had high hopes that the Thunderace could topple the FireBlade, but unfortunately was to be disappointed.

On paper at least, the Thunderace looked like a strong contender. The foundation of the design was the old FZR1000 EXUP engine, although thoroughly revised and clothed in a new set of stylish bodywork. So the 1002cc motor from the FZR was re-tuned, now putting out an impressive 108kW (145bhp), and mounted in a new aluminium frame, based on the YZF750's design, with new suspension and brakes.

The new bike was much lighter than the FZR at 198kg (437lb), but was still some way off the FireBlade's sylph-like 184kg (406lb). It felt much bigger and longer too, and was simply not as dynamic or as sporty as the Honda, especially on track or on tight twisty roads.

On the right roads, and in the right hands though, the Thunderace is immensely fast. The EXUP engine is strong all the way through the rev range, and the delivery is so torquey that five gears are all that a rider needs. The front brakes were a revelation at the launch – the one-piece four-piston Sumitomo calipers have since become standard Yamaha sportsbike fare, but their power, progression and feel were miles ahead of the 1996 opposition.

The Thunderace's conventional suspension has a lot of work to do controlling the mass and speed of the bike, but it never feels anything less than stable, even in fast sweeping bends.

The steering is slower than smaller machines, but contributes to stability.

The Thunderace was relegated to a sports-touring role by the introduction of the R1, in 1998, although its combination of performance and comfort have ensured it remains a strong seller.

Top speed:	274km/h (170mph)
Engine type:	1002cc, l/c inline-four, 20-valve, DOHC
Maximum power:	108kW (145bhp) at 10,000rpm
Frame type:	aluminium twin-spar
Tyre sizes:	front 120/70 17, rear 180/55 17
Final drive:	chain
Gearbox:	five-speed
Weight:	198kg (437lb)

Yamaha YZF-R1

Yamaha's YZF-R1 revolutionized the open-class sports market when it first appeared in 1998. The first riding reports spoke of an incredible blend of tiny size, light weight and power, all backing up the incredible on-paper specification of the R1.

Almost every part of the R1 was new. Cunning design and advanced materials allowed the 20-valve inline-four engine to be extremely short, narrow and light. The crankshaft and gearbox shafts are arranged in a triangular arrangement, with the gearbox input shaft sitting above the crank, permitting a shorter engine/gearbox unit. Magnesium covers, forged pistons and a single-piece upper-crankcase/cylinder unit all further help weight loss.

A variant of the Yamaha Deltabox aluminium frame, called Deltabox II, is extremely short and stiff, and uses the engine as a stressed component to add strength without weight. That short engine design permits a longer swingarm, which pushes more weight over the front end, and improves rear wheel traction under power, while retaining an ultra-short 1395mm (55in) wheelbase.

The front forks also used new design concepts – extra travel was incorporated, which allows the front wheel to stay in contact with the ground for longer under hard acceleration. The front brakes had already been seen on the Thunderace, but worked even better on the lightweight R1.

The R1 remained at the top of the sportsbike pile until 2001, when the superior power of Suzuki's GSX-R1000 deposed it. For 2002, the R1 received a comprehensive update, including fuel-injection, less weight and better brakes and handling. The all-new fuel-injection system uses a sliding piston valve design, similar to that on CV carbs, to match airflow velocity to engine requirements. The latest black-finished Deltabox III frame is lighter than before, but is 30 per cent stiffer.

The 2002 R1 was still behind the GSX-R on outright power and all-up weight, but its superb handling and excellent fuel-injection helped redress the balance.

Top speed:	290km/h (175mph)
Engine type:	998cc, l/c inline-four, 20-valve, DOHC
Maximum power:	113kW (152bhp) at 10,500rpm
Frame type:	aluminium twin-spar
Tyre sizes:	front 120/70 17, rear 190/50 17
Final drive:	chain
Gearbox:	six-speed
Weight:	174kg (384lb)

Yamaha BT1100 Bulldog

The Bulldog is a rather curious motorcycle, with a somewhat confused identity. Styled like a naked, aggressive musclebike, which looks like it could take on Ducati's Monster or Buell's X-1, the Bulldog actually offers rather mediocre performance. Its exposed V-twin engine is borrowed from the XV1100 Drag Star, and offers just 48kW (65bhp). Chassis-wise, a tasteful steel-tube perimeter frame snakes around the top of the engine, R1-type front brakes are fitted, and the hunched fuel tank makes the Italian-styled Bulldog look like a short, taut machine. It's attractive too, with a neat flyscreen and high-quality detail finish. But again, the performance is more akin to a cruiser than an aggressive musclebike.

Top speed:	185km/h (115mph)
Engine type:	1063cc, a/c 75° V-twin, four-valve, SOHC
Maximum power:	48kW (65bhp) at 5500rpm
Frame type:	steel-tube perimeter
Tyre sizes:	front 120/70 17, rear 170/60 17
Final drive:	shaft
Gearbox:	five-speed
Weight:	229kg (505lb)

Yamaha XVS-1100 Drag Star

Yamaha's 1100 Drag Star replaced the firm's long-running 1100 Virago in 1998. Styled like its smaller 650 namesake, the 1100 used the Virago's V-twin engine, but with a restyled low-rider chassis. The rear end looks like a hardtail chopper design, but has a hidden monoshock swingarm and shaft final drive. Conventional front forks are kicked out to give radical chopper looks, and a narrow 46cm (18in) front wheel is mounted with twin front discs and double piston brake calipers. The seat is low and combines with the pullback handlebars and forward footpegs to create a traditional chopper riding position. There's little protection from the wind though, and the wide bars aggravate the wind blast on the rider's chest.

Top speed:	177km/h (110mph)
Engine type:	1063cc, a/c 75° V-twin, four-valve, SOHC
Maximum power:	46kW (62bhp) at 5750rpm
Frame type:	steel-tube cradle
Tyre sizes:	front 110/90 18, rear 170/80 15
Final drive:	shaft
Gearbox:	five-speed
Weight:	259kg (571lb)

Yamaha VMX1200 V-Max

One of motorcycling's legendary names, the V-Max has become a byword for explosive acceleration and power. First launched in the USA in 1984 (it wasn't officially imported to Britain until 1991) the V-Max quickly established a reputation for scary power, and equally scary handling. The engine had immense power and torque, more than sufficient to overcome the chassis and brakes.

The engine is a transverse V-four, 16-valve, liquid-cooled design, with a unique intake system. Over 6000rpm, valves open in the inlet manifold, allowing each cylinder to breathe through two carburettors rather than one. This 'V-Boost' system supplies an extra burst of power and torque, transforming the V-Max into a screaming drag-racer, and boosting the maximum power to 104kW (140bhp), amazing performance for an early 1980s design.

The V-Max's extreme power would be enough to overwhelm some modern sportsbike chassis, but in a 1980s custom chassis it can be truly scary for the rider. The front disc brakes lack both power and feel while the narrow front forks and unsophisticated twin rear shocks quickly lose control of wheel movement in fast corners.

The double cradle steel-tube frame is too weak to handle all the power, and chassis flex further upsets cornering, causing wallow and weave whenever the pace is raised. Stronger brakes were fitted in 1993, but made little difference to the V-Max's chassis performance.

But in a straight line, the V-Max is an awesome performer, with enough power to spin its wide 150-section rear tyre away from a standing start. A five-speed gearbox and heavy-duty shaft final drive get the power from the engine to the cast aluminium rear wheel.

The design of the V-Max is unconventional in many ways. The fuel tank lives under the seat, and access is via a flap in the seat. An instrument console mounted on the dummy fuel tank houses the tacho, temperature gauge and indicator lights, while the chrome-plated speedo is mounted above the headlight.

Top speed:	232km/h (144mph)
Engine type:	1198cc, l/c 90° V-four, 16-valve, DOHC
Maximum power:	104kW (140bhp) at 8500rpm
Frame type:	steel-tube double cradle
Tyre sizes:	front 110/90 18, rear 150/90 15
Final drive:	shaft
Gearbox:	five-speed
Weight:	262kg (576lb)

Yamaha FJR1300

Yamaha's touring range was rather thin throughout the 1990s. Only the XJ900 Diversion offered any touring ability, but it couldn't match modern tourers like Honda's Pan European. So for 2001, Yamaha introduced the FJR1300, one of the most powerful and advanced tourers on the market. Much of the spec sheet reads like a sportsbike: a twin-spar aluminium frame, 107kW (145bhp) fuel-injected engine, one-piece four-piston R1 brake calipers and adjustable suspension. But all this technology was contained inside a large touring fairing, with comfortable, upright riding position, shaft drive and integrated hard luggage design. The FJR thus combines sporting performance with touring convenience.

Top speed:	249km/h (155mph)
Engine type:	1298cc, l/c inline-four, 16-valve, DOHC
Maximum power:	107kW (144bhp) at 8000rpm
Frame type:	aluminium twin-spar
Tyre sizes:	front 120/70 17, rear 180/55 17
Final drive:	shaft
Gearbox:	five-speed
Weight:	237kg (522lb)

Yamaha XJR1300

Yamaha's XJR1300 is a classic naked musclebike design, made special by some high-spec chassis components. The XJR engine evolved from the previous XJR1200's motor in 1998, although the air-cooled 16-valve in-line four traces its history back much further – first seen in 1200cc form in the 1986 FJ1200, which in turn was developed from the FJ1100 of 1984. The strong, torquey motor is installed in a straightforward steel-tube chassis with conventional front forks and a twin-shock rear swingarm. The rear shocks are Öhlins, which Yamaha owns, and their trademark yellow springs give a dash of colour to the XJR's back end, as do the blue-centred R1-type front brake calipers, which give strong, progressive stopping power.

Top speed:	233km/h (145mph)
Engine type:	1251cc, a/c inline-four, 16-valve, DOHC
Maximum power:	79kW (106bhp) at 8000rpm
Frame type:	steel-tube double cradle
Tyre sizes:	front 120/70 17, rear 180/55 17
Final drive:	chain
Gearbox:	five-speed
Weight:	224kg (493lb)

Yamaha XVZ1300 Royal Star

The Royal Star is a massive, retro-styled touring cruiser powered by a larger, de-tuned version of the 1198cc V-Max engine. The V-4 engine, which makes 104kW (140bhp) in the V-Max, produces around half that figure in the Royal Star. Yamaha has altered the engine's carburation and timing to move the power further down the rev range: the peak torque figure of 82ft lb is produced at just 3500rpm. Having said that, the Royal Star is incredibly heavy, at 328kg (723lb), limiting its dynamic appeal. Beefy fork shrouds, extensive chrome-plating and spoked wheels are all authentic cruiser-style. Its touring abilities are further helped by the low-maintenance shaft drive and 18-litre (4 gal) fuel tank.

Top speed:	193km/h (120mph)
Engine type:	1294cc, l/c 90° V-4, 16-valve, DOHC
Maximum power:	55kW (74bhp) at 4750rpm
Frame type:	steel-tube double cradle
Tyre sizes:	front 150/80 19, rear 150/90 15
Final drive:	shaft
Gearbox:	five-speed
Weight:	328kg (723lb)

Yamaha XV1600 Wild Star

Yamaha's largest-capacity machine, the Wild Star is a massive piece of engineering. A huge V-twin motor produces almost 100ft lb of torque at barely over tickover. The design of the engine blends old and new – it's a pushrod-valve air-cooled motor, but with a unique four-valve pushrod design, and Kevlar belt final drive. The styling is pure retro lowrider: valanced mudguards, hardtail-styled rear suspension and fork shrouds. Pullback handlebars, forward footboards and a low-slung seat put the rider in the perfect cruising position, although provision for a pillion is minimal. For 2001 Yamaha released an even larger version in the US – the XV1700 Road Star Warrior used a large 1670cc version of the Wild Star engine.

Top speed:	177km/h (110mph)
Engine type:	1602cc, a/c 48° V-twin, eight-valve, OHV
Maximum power:	47kW (63bhp) at 4000rpm
Frame type:	steel-tube double cradle
Tyre sizes:	front 130/90 16, rear 150/80 16
Final drive:	belt
Gearbox:	five-speed
Weight:	307kg (677lb)

Glossary

ABS – Antilock braking system. Uses computer-controlled sensors and pressure valves to release hydraulic brake pressure when a wheel locks, preventing skidding.

Aluminium twin spar – Design of frame with two aluminium extruded spars, normally welded to cast steering and swingarm pivot points.

Backbone frame – Frame design which uses a large single tube from the swingarm pivot to the steering head pivot, hanging the engine below it. Also known as spine frame.

Bevel drive – Mechanical arrangement to turn a shaft drive through 90°. Used on some camshaft drives as well as shaft final drive systems.

BHP – Brake horsepower. A measure of power, equivalent to 550ft lb/s or 745.7 watts.

Camchain – Chain fitted inside an engine which turns the camshaft via a sprocket on the crankshaft.

Camshaft – Rotating shaft with cam profiles machined in, which push engine valves open and closed as it turns.

Carburettor – Mechanical device to introduce atomized fuel into the airflow into the engine.

CBS – Combined braking system. Used by Honda to link front and rear braking circuits via hydraulic hoses and control valves.

Compression damping – A system for absorbing suspension movement on the compression (upward) stroke of a wheel. Normally uses oil forced through small holes.

Compression ratio – The ratio of the volume of an engine cylinder at bottom dead centre to the volume at top dead centre.

CV Carburettors – Constant Velocity carburettors use a vacuum diaphragm to control airflow into the engine.

Desmodromic – Valve operating system which uses cams to positively close as well as open engine valves. Favoured by Ducati.

DOHC – Double overhead camshaft. Engine layout with two overhead cams, one for inlet valves, one for exhaust valves.

Double cradle frame – Frame design which uses two rails running down from the steering head in front of the engine and back to the swingarm pivot plates.

EFI – Electronic fuel-injection. Computerized system which uses electronic solenoid injectors and an ECU to deliver precisely metered fuel to the engine.

ECU – Electronic control unit. The 'brain' of an EFI system, which uses sensors (temperature, engine position, throttle opening) to determine how much fuel to inject into the engine, and when.

EXUP – Exhaust Ultimate Powervalve. Yamaha's system for controlling pressure pulses within a four-stroke exhaust to improve mid-range power.

Floating disc – Brake disc which is attached to its carrier by loose dowels. This allows the disc to expand and contract as it heats up in operation without cracking.

Four-piston caliper – Brake caliper design which uses two hydraulic pistons either side of the brake disc to clamp the brake pad on to the disc.

Ft lb – Foot-pounds force. A measure of torque, or twisting force. One ft lb is equivalent to 1.356 newton metres.

Inline-four – Most common form of sportsbike engine. Has four cylinders arranged in a line.

Master cylinder – Hydraulic control cylinder which is operated by hand or foot lever. Uses a piston to pressurize hydraulic fluid and operate hydraulic pistons in brake calipers.

Monoshock – Suspension system which uses one shock absorber to control (normally) a rear swingarm. Can use a rising rate linkage, which increases shock movement as the wheel moves, or a linear linkage.

OHC – Overhead cam. Type of engine layout where the camshaft is located above the combustion chamber.

OHV – Overhead valve. Engine layout where the valves are above the combustion chamber operated by long pushrods linking them to a camshaft next to the crankshaft.

Radial tyres – Modern tyre construction type which uses radial construction threads running from one side of the tyre to the other. Allows a lighter, cooler running tyre carcass.

Ram-airbox – A sealed airbox with intakes positioned at the front of the motorcycle. As road speed increases, wind blast pressurizes the airbox slightly, giving a power increase.

Rebound damping – A system for absorbing suspension movement on the rebound (downward) stroke of a wheel.

This system normally uses oil forced through small holes.

Ride height adjustment – Method of adjusting the position of a suspension unit in relation to the chassis, which moves the chassis up and down.

Slide carburettor – Slide carburettors use a simple piston valve connected to the throttle to control airflow into the engine.

SOHC – Single overhead camshaft. Engine layout with one camshaft for inlet and exhaust valves.

Spring preload – Means of adjusting the static load on a suspension spring. Uses a threaded or cammed collar.

Swingarm – Pivoting fork which allows a (usually) rear wheel to move up and down over bumps. Controlled by one or two suspension units.

Tachometer – Instrument to display engine speed.

Upside-down fork – Type of telescopic suspension fork where the inner chromed stanchion tube attaches to the front wheel, and the outer slider tube is mounted at the top, attached to the steering yokes.

V-four – Engine layout with two pairs of cylinder arranged at an angle to each other in a 'V' or 'L' shape, commonly 90°.

V-twin – Engine layout with two cylinders arranged at an angle to each other in a V-shape.

Wheelbase – Measurement of length between the points where front and rear wheel touch the ground, in a line down from the wheel axles.

Yokes – Pair of clamps that attach the telescopic forks to the steering axle that passes through the steering head.

Index